Losing Her Finding Me

Losing Her Finding Me

A MOTHER'S STORY
OF ESTRANGEMENT AND SELF-DISCOVERY

Michelle Rohlf

REDEMPTION PRESS

ISBN 13: 978-1-64645-653-6 (Paperback)
   978-1-64645-655-0 (ePub)
   978-1-64645-654-3 (Mobi)
   978-1-64645-556-0 (Audiobook)

LCCN: 2022907082

Dedication

I dedicate this book to God,
because it was His idea.
And to Marilee, for being
the boots on the ground,
pushing me through to the end.

Contents

PART 2 FINDING ME

Acknowledgments

My gratitude to Redemption Press, especially to Athena Dean Holtz who thought my story was intriguing and sent me to the website, to Jennifer Fedler, my project manager, and Dori Harrell, the managing editor, for their kindness and direction through the publishing process.

Thanks and praise to God for giving me the gift of writing, to Jesus for saving me, and to the Holy Spirit who is with me always, reminding me who I am and whose I am.

Many thanks to all who prayed for me and encouraged me through this last year. I was bathed in God's provision and direction.

To my dear sister-friend Marilee, for her undying devotion to me and this project. Her persistence and commitment to me and this book helped me be persistent and committed. I am honored to call the Masons' Plumcreek my second home because I always feel welcome. A special shout-out to Marilee's husband, Greg, who fed me yummy smoked meat and was a sensible voice in the storm of emotions.

To Pam at Pam's Grounds for Coffee in Clearfield,

Utah, where many words were written, and many meals were eaten.

To New York Times Best Selling author Dan Schilling, who took his time to consult a new writer when so many others I reached out to wouldn't.

Thanks to Sarah for consulting on the cover of the book. Her advice was invaluable.

To Neal, Linda, Robyn, and Karen, who read the early manuscript and encouraged me to publish.

To Judi, who was the honest, tough, straight-talking, and compassionate sponsor I needed. She was instrumental in my recovery.

To the women who mentored me in my Christian walk: Joy, Susan, Mary Kay, and Sandra. Your words and wisdom forever echo in my mind.

To the Rickman family, Victor, Connor, and Blythe, for permitting me to use part of their story. I marvel at their courage.

To Dazii, who took my head shots. I'm so proud of you!

To my husband, Lance, who is the best man I know. His commitment to God and to his family is remarkable. He consistently loves me, encourages me, and points me to the Savior. Thank you, Lance, for speaking the truth, even when I'm being a pill. I love you!

To my parents, Robert and Sandra Rickman, for taking care of me, loving me, and modeling the love and service of others. I miss you every day.

Part 1

Losing Her

Chapter 1

The Worst

"You don't think we can work this out? That they'll come around? Why . . . I mean, how—you think it's over forever?"

I started to panic as the possibility set in. My husband, Lance, was the unemotional one, the logical one, the let's-take-a-breath-and-figure-this-out one.

What. Was. Happening?

Lance walked into the living room and sat down next to me.

He didn't speak for a long time, and then, "Michelle, they called us liars in our own home. They have been keeping that baby away from us all year, and now they have accused us of things we have never done. There is no coming back from this. We have no defense." He pulled in a breath as he swiped at unwelcome tears.

"But we didn't do those things," I said. "There's got to be something we can do. Something we can say. We have got to change this! How could this happen to us? We were good parents. We were amazing grandparents. I don't understand how this is happening to us."

I was still not crying. There *were* tears for me. I was in shock. Daughters don't do this to their parents. Children don't do this to their parents, period. I couldn't believe Naomi would do this to me. Okay, maybe to *me*, because she had been mad at me ever since her grandmother died, but not to Lance! She *loved* her dad. How could she do this to us? We had always supported her and encouraged her, and we'd given her every opportunity under the sun. Even if we had done something wrong, how could she walk out that door and not have a little grace for her parents being human? This was crazy, it couldn't be real, it couldn't be forever . . . but it looked like it just might be.

Chapter 2

The Beginning

The day I met my sweet baby Naomi was the day I came alive.

The moment the maternity nurse put her into my arms, all the pieces of my existence came into focus. I had literally *grown* a best friend who would accept me and love me forever. It was a miracle. *She* was a miracle! But that was not really the beginning.

I was born in the spring of 1963 and raised in the small town of Kaysville, Utah. Our house backed up to the Wasatch Mountains. A creek flowed out of those mountains, dividing our yard from the neighbor's. We lived on a hill, where we could see the Great Salt Lake and Antelope Island from our front room window. It was a lovely place to grow up. And no, I wasn't Mormon, but practically everyone else was.

I had one sibling, Dick, who was four years older. He

did not like me and vacillated between ignoring me and making my life miserable. He made fun of me incessantly, and when he was nice to me, it was to manipulate me into doing something for his entertainment. He tricked me into drinking soap water. He pretended to be interested in my gymnastics, asking me to show him some moves just so he could drink the soda we were sharing. I could go on and on about our sibling rivalry, but my brother says I should save the brother stories for another time. If you have siblings, you have stories.

I'm not clear how much time I spent with my maternal grandma, but I have specific early memories of her and her treatment of me. I don't want to use the word *abuse*, but she wasn't nice to me. She criticized me often, and she favored my brother, which made it even worse.

When I was five years old, I stayed with Grandma and Grandpa for two weeks. It's the earliest memory I have of Grandma, and I think the reason it stuck is because of this event. I was standing in the kitchen with Grandma when we heard the door open, and my mom called out:

"Hi! It's Mom! I have a surprise for you!" She came to the kitchen door and placed a little black bundle of fur on the floor.

"Her name is Candy, because you love candy," she said.

I scooped up the puppy and hugged her close. She licked my face and wiggled around so much I almost dropped her.

"Thank you, Mom!" I said as I juggled the puppy in my dimpled arms.

I looked up at my mom, beaming with gratitude. I had a friend! Someone who would love me forever. My mom knew exactly what I needed—a sweet, fluffy, attentive friend. Such a wise mom.

Not long after Mom got there, Grandma asked if we wanted breakfast.

"Sure!" I said. "Can I have a doughnut?"

Okay, I'm not really sure what I asked for, but it had to be something sugary, because Grandma got really irritated with me.

"All you ever want is sugar. Okay! You are grounded from food all day. Today, all you can eat is sugar. Maybe once you eat sweets all day, you'll stop wanting them all the time."

I wasn't that sad about it. I didn't care for her delivery, but I was a kid, and getting permission to eat candy all day was a pretty cool thing . . . or so I thought. By dinnertime I was hungry for real food.

My dad and grandpa were grilling hamburgers, and the smell beckoned me. I told my grandma I wanted real food, and she just berated me, reminding me of the choice I had made that morning.

Did I mention I was five? I was five. Five years old, and I was being punished for wanting a doughnut.

Anyway, I went to my mom and asked her if I could please have a hamburger, and she talked to my grandma. I guess they came to an agreement, because I had dinner with the family, and yes, I had a hamburger.

Best. Hamburger. Ever!

Grandma had her favorite grandkids, and I wasn't one of them. It seemed to me she favored the ones who were pretty and thin . . . maybe? She made a character judgment about me that I didn't have self-control or I was lazy or something. She was disciplined, strong, and independent, and she made it known to others around her how she felt about you if you were not. Self-control mattered the most to my grandma, and being thin was one obvious indicator of that. I was not acceptable.

No matter what I did, it was never enough to please her. I don't know why I kept trying, but I did. I wanted to be loved by her. I wanted her to accept me and think I was awesome. I wanted her to treat me like the other grandkids, so I kept trying and kept failing. She would never get past the idea that I was fat. I was not fat. Maybe she thought she was preventing me from getting fat.

Her message was clear in the way she treated my grandpa. She would criticize him about being fat or eating too much or dropping food on his shirt. She would do it in front of everyone. I felt sorry for him.

One time when I was a little older, after ten minutes of her smattering us both with critical comments, my normally quiet grandpa said sternly, "Ruth! We've had enough of the fat comments."

The room fell silent. Everyone stopped moving, as I remember it, and the comments stopped too. I'll never forget him for standing up for me at that moment. People who should have didn't defend me. He did. He spoke for me when I couldn't speak for myself. I will always love him for that.

One time when I was almost thirty years old, I lost over a hundred pounds. I went from size 38 to size 16, and when I saw my grandma, she didn't say a word to me. I started talking about my weight loss, hoping to finagle a compliment or an acknowledgment out of her, and all I got was "You still have a ways to go."

Yeah, well, I guess I do. I got nothing. What did I expect? Something. I guess I expected something. I should have known better, but I didn't. I am the eternal optimist, always giving people chances to disappoint me, and that was what they did—disappoint me.

Chapter 3

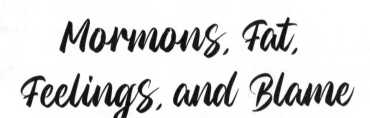

Mormons, Fat, Feelings, and Blame

Okay, so back to growing up in a town full of Mormons. Please don't take this to mean I think all Mormons are bad. I think what happened to me would happen with any group where there's an outsider, especially where that "outsider" feels like an outsider even in the intimate circle of family. I already had plenty of evidence to feed the idea that I was not enough—not good enough, smart enough, cute enough, thin enough . . .

But I do have many stories where I was rejected because I wasn't Mormon. Probably the most hurtful was when I was eleven years old. I had two friends who were in most of my classes, and we were close. We spent the night at one another's houses, and as far as I knew, we were all best friends.

One day at school, they said they couldn't be my friends anymore because I wasn't Mormon. I walked into my next class, laid my head on my desk, and cried. Another thing I was not, and another reason I was unacceptable.

My dad and brother would tease me about being fat. Or really, they'd tease me about anything. If it wasn't about fat, it'd be about something else, but since I was a little fluffier than many super-skinny girls around me, they took the easy route to get at me.

We'd be having a perfectly nice evening watching TV as a family when they would start in on me. It just took one of them to start, and then the other would join in. It was an opportunity for my brother to bond with my dad, so he never missed a chance to chime in or to get things rolling. Most of the time the teasing ended with me crying and running to my room while the rest of the family stayed out in the living room finishing the TV program together.

One time my mom got up to come after me, and I heard my dad yell down the hall, "Sure, go after her—you baby her too much! We are just teasing her!"

Mom didn't like being yelled at—who would? Eventually, she stopped coming after me. She stopped getting involved at all, which left me to deal with the abuse on my own.

Emotions were not welcome in our home unless they were coming from Dad. He was the only one allowed to express anger or frustration. The rest of us were allowed to express happiness—that was all, just happiness. Anything else was met with disgust.

One day I came home after saying goodbye to my friend, who was going on a Mormon mission to New Zealand. He was going to be gone for two years, and I was sad.

I came home with tears in my eyes, and my dad said, "Did Chad get off okay?"

"Yeah." My voice broke and tears pushed their way past my eyelids.

"Well, it's not like he's leaving forever!" he gruffed. "You don't have to keep crying about it!"

"It just happened!" I yelled as I brushed the tears away. "He left thirty minutes ago. Can I just have a minute to be sad?" I slammed out of the room before he could berate me.

That was the story of my life at home. Emotions were a no-no, and I was *not* good at hiding them or not having them. Yet another thing I didn't do right.

One time I was blamed for getting alcohol for a bunch of kids, because the Mormon parents couldn't believe their kids could misbehave in this way without the non-Mormon being the instigator. Another time one of my friends was brought home by a policeman at 2:00 a.m. She had been picked up for underage drinking and public intoxication with the bishop's daughter.

The next morning, I talked to my friend, and she said her mom asked if I had been with them. I hadn't seen or hung around that friend in years. It had to be the non-Mormon corrupting the innocent Mormon kids. It wasn't me!

One time I was blamed for telling my little cousin the facts of life. I hardly even knew what they were, and I don't know why she lied to my aunt or what she told her I said, but I got blamed. I could never prove otherwise.

I could go on and on about all the times I've been unjustly blamed for things I didn't do. I could tell stories of friendships lost because of stupid, irrational reasons and situations so puzzling that I am still shaking my head in disbelief. I am *that* person. The dog that gets kicked when you've had a bad day at work, or the person you yell at because you can't yell at your spouse. I'm the one. It's me! The scapegoat, the whipping girl, the fall gal.

I don't know how I got that distinction, although my husband has a theory. He thinks that people beat me up because I am so happy all the time and I don't fight back. I guess that could be true, especially for those who are not happy themselves. What's worse than having a perpetually happy person around to remind you how unhappy you are?

One time when I was training a bunch of new employees, one of the girls told me later, when we became friends, she couldn't stand me the first week. She was so miserable because she didn't want to be in the training, and from the first day, she'd sit there mystified, asking herself, "What's *she* so happy about?"

I guess that could be annoying.

When I was young, I was so naïve I generally didn't know that someone was being rude unless it was extremely obvious. I so wanted to be loved and accepted that I chose to believe everyone was kind and had the best intentions.

Whew. Have I learned that's not true. Although I still start there, it doesn't take as long to convince me otherwise.

Chapter 4

Marriage No. 1
The Kevin Years

I met Naomi's dad in 1984, when I was twenty-one. I had just lost my best friend to diabetes, and I was adrift. I didn't have a job, and I was hanging around a girl named Brandy, who partied all night, slept all day, and wrote bad checks. She was practically living at my house until my dad called us out on it.

We would go dancing at Hill Air Force Base or at the clubs in Salt Lake City. I was never comfortable in those situations, but it was something to do, and I was drifting. I was afraid of men. I was afraid of intimacy. I felt uneasy when a man made it known to me he wanted me in *that* way. It felt like a lie. I felt like they were lying and they really didn't want *me*. They just wanted sex, and they were hoping I'd give it to them. I never felt like a man could want me for me, and looking back, I realize the ones who did want me for me, I ran away from as fast as my legs could carry me.

Which brings me to Chuck.

I met Chuck at one of the dance clubs in the city. He wasn't the most confident guy, and he was average on the eyes, but he was nice. Brandy had hooked up with his friend, and they asked us back to their place to "watch a movie." It didn't take long before Brandy and her beau had disappeared, leaving me and Chuck alone. We talked for a while, and then we started to kiss. I was a little tipsy, so I let things go further than I probably would have normally, but when it came down to it—you know—*it*, we stopped. Chuck asked for my number before I left, and he called me the next day and asked me out to dinner. I was excited!

I went out with Chuck for a couple of months. I enjoyed his company, and we had things in common. He was sweet and respectful, and he really liked me. He treated me the way a woman should be treated, and that was just not acceptable. I was not worthy, and I knew it. It was time for me to sabotage it.

After an evening of partying with his friends and his roommate, Kevin, I ended up spending the night at his house. Later that night, I was walking down the hall to the bathroom when Kevin came out of the bathroom draped in a towel. We giggled and moved around each other so I could get to the door, and I noticed he was staring at me. I had been a fan of his eyes from the moment I met him—he had these big, sky-blue eyes—but this time they were zeroed in on me.

I turned around, grabbed the door, and closed it with him watching from the hall. I was in love—or was it lust?

I didn't care. I wanted that man, and I was going to do whatever it took to get him.

It didn't take much.

A couple of nights later, Chuck, Kevin, and I were up partying when Kevin and I went to run an errand. I can't remember what it was. We stopped at my house on the way home, and Kevin started pawing at me. Well, it didn't take much persuading, and we ended up having sex.

Chuck called soon after and asked where we were. I lied and gave him some story about having to pick something up at home, or a flat tire, or something. I felt awful, but I also felt elated. I was in over my head with this Kevin, and I was dating Chuck.

Okay, now what, idiot?

I'm not the kind of person who can hold things in or tell lies or remember the lies I told, so I knew I had to come clean to Chuck. He was such a sweet man, and I had to not only tell him I wanted another man, *but his roommate*! They'd been friends for years, and Kevin didn't have many friends, and now he was going to lose one. Not good.

I called ahead and asked Chuck if I could see him. He knew what was coming because Kevin had already talked to him. He was sitting on the couch, drinking and angry.

I crossed the room and stood in front of him. "I am so sorry about this. I didn't mean for it to happen. I really liked you."

"Yeah, well, that doesn't matter now, does it?" he snarled. "You obviously didn't like me enough."

I looked down at my hands. "I am sorry, Chuck. You are a really great guy. I think I suck at this relationship stuff."

"Okay, fine. Now get out. I'm going to drink a lot and work on my car." He stood up and started for the back door.

"Bye—I am so sorry." I watched him leave.

I felt like such a pig. He was a good guy, and as I look back, I think he really liked me. I could have had a future with him. He was responsible, had a job, was ambitious and confident. Kevin didn't have any of those things. He had a low-level job, a beat-up truck, and two DUIs to his name. He didn't have any confidence or self-respect. He was a mess, and I intentionally picked him over a healthy, responsible guy.

I should have seen the warning signs, but I was too weakened by the damage that had been done to me. I didn't believe I was worthy of a decent guy. Whenever a man would compliment me, I didn't believe him. Chuck would say nice things. Kevin never did. Getting a compliment out of Kevin was like keeping the beer out of his hands . . . impossible!

My dad was another man in my life who seldom commented on my beauty. He was liberal with praise for other women but sparse on anything for me or my super-cute mom. From a very young age, I was bombarded by my dad's observations of other women, whether they were on TV, on the street, at a party, or if they were one of my friends or a friend's mom. No woman was safe from my dad's scrutiny.

About a woman crossing the street in front of us as we waited at the stoplight: "Wow! Show it off, sister!"

Beautiful actress on the television: "She is one beautiful woman. Such class!"

Any shapely woman: "She sure is stacked!"

It went on and on. Then when my brother got old enough to notice girls, he would join in, which just intensified the problem.

It's funny how things affect you. Hearing those comments for all those years told me, as a little girl becoming a young lady, "beauty" looked thin, blond, and stacked, and I wasn't even one of those. I was short, stubby, not stacked, and brunette. I was not going to be that kind of woman. I was going to be the other kind, the ones who have a "good personality."

Now that I'm old and gray, I can see I picked Kevin over Chuck because I believed Chuck was a liar. He gave me respect, and I didn't believe I deserved it. He thought I was pretty, and I knew it wasn't so. I didn't believe I was good enough for him, so I found someone who was just as damaged as me—and we deserved each other.

Kevin was a quiet guy. He didn't talk—hardly ever. I can't believe I considered him as a life mate because I was *always* talking and *always* wanted to bounce different ideas around about life, the universe, physics, human behavior . . . you get the point.

Whenever I asked Kevin his opinion, he failed to have one. He would just say he didn't know and turn back to his wrestling on TV or grab a beer—or me. His interests were exactly those things: wrestling, alcohol, and sex. I can't believe I settled for it, but I did. I settled, and I married him, and I even had a baby with him.

We moved in together within a week of knowing each other, and we lived together for two and half years. We got along pretty well because Kevin was passive, and he did whatever I wanted to do. He had no opinions and seemed perfectly happy with working, beer, and sex. He didn't challenge me.

I went with him to court as he faced the consequences of the two DUIs he had gotten before meeting me. I can't remember what he had to do besides pay a fine and give up his license. I thought that was the end of that, but why I would think that is beyond me.

Kevin asked me to marry him, I'm sure after I told him he was going to ask me, and I told him I would not marry him unless he stopped drinking. I knew I didn't want to marry an alcoholic, especially with all the drama that came with it, so he agreed he'd stop. He quit six months before the wedding, and those were the best months of our relationship.

I wanted to spend the night before the wedding apart so we'd be excited to see each other the next day, so I stayed at my parents' house. We met up at the rehearsal breakfast the next morning.

The rehearsal breakfast was in the same little refurbished Victorian place my mom had booked for the wedding, and both of our families were there that morning. Kevin arrived with his best man, and I was excited to see him, to show him my pretty new dress.

"Good morning!" I stepped in to kiss him.

He kissed me back and embraced me. "Good morning." He parroted back.

A familiar aroma assaulted me. I wasn't even sure I smelled it so much as felt it sort of envelop me. The feeling started right below my sternum and made its way to my heart, making it beat loud and fast. Then my head started to spin.

I stepped back out of his embrace, and he saw it. He knew I knew. My mind was going as fast as my heart, and I couldn't finish a thought.

I hissed. "You've been drinking. I told you I wouldn't marry you . . ." I must've whispered it to him, because no one glanced our way. In my mind I was screaming.

I looked around and took in all the people. Parker had come from Nevada, Mary from Vegas. My aunts had come from Colorado, and my friend Chad from Arizona. *What am I going to do? Should I call it off? What is my dad going to say?*

Kevin tried to grab my arm as I stepped away from him. He tried to talk to me. "I just had a bachelor party drink. It was the last time, I promise." He sounded desperate.

I stared at him, and he let me go. *I can't do it. I can't call it off.* I knew I should. I knew this was not the right decision. *I can't disappoint Dad and embarrass Mom—I'm going to have to go through with it.*

"I can't believe you did this, Kevin. I told you." I tried to keep my voice at an acceptable level. Tried to keep from getting hysterical.

He pleaded with me. I could see it in his messed-up alcoholic eyes. *I can't believe I'm doing this. I'm actually going to marry this man. What an idiot!*

The wedding went as planned, except that Kevin drank the whole night, even though we didn't have any alcohol at the wedding. I guess his best man smuggled it in for him—what a friend.

The wedding night was a bust. My brother gave us a suite at the Little America in Salt Lake City. The room was lovely and had a beautiful view of the city. I went into the bathroom to get ready and came out to a snoring husband. I turned off the lights and got into bed.

What did I get myself into?

Chapter 5

The Honeymoon Is Over

Kevin never stopped drinking again. His favorite thing to do was to drive around town and drink beer in his truck, probably because he knew I wouldn't approve of him drinking in our home. Sometimes he would stay out all night without calling—drinking and driving. When he finally made it home, I would be so angry! Once I knew he was alive, I'd pack my things and leave. This happened over and over again, which I now know is not uncommon for the home of an addict. I stuck with him because no one else would want me, and I didn't want to be alone.

Five months after we were married, I flew to California to see my friend Patty and her husband. She was pregnant with her first child. I flew out the Friday after Thanksgiving and came home the following Monday.

When I got home, Kevin sat me down and told me he had gotten another DUI. I was *so* angry that I screamed at him, stomped around, and slept on the couch that night. The next day, he sent me flowers at work. Even though I said they wouldn't fix the problem, it put a Band-Aid on it until the next one.

Yes, I said the next one.

Well, let's see. We were married in June, and he got his third DUI in November and his fourth in December. Yep! You read it right. Two more DUIs, five weeks apart, for a total of four.

The last one came at Christmastime. Kevin was working late, and I was home alone watching *The Sound of Music*, dancing and singing my way through each song, when the phone rang.

"Hellooo!" I answered musically. (*Doe . . . a deer, a female deer!*)

"Michelle, I need you to come get me."

"Oh, hi! What? What happened? Oh, no, did your truck break down again?" I said, still dancing to the musical musings of the Von Trapp family as they hung from trees in clothes made of curtains—those silly Von Trapp children! They make me smile every time.

"Ahhhh . . . no . . . I'm in jail. I'm at the courthouse, downtown," Kevin whispered.

"What . . . how . . . where . . . *What is wrong with you?*" I shouted.

To be honest, I don't remember what I did next. I do remember walking into the courthouse to pick him up, and I remember crying and screaming at him while I drove him home. I was so out of my mind, he asked me if he should drive. Ha!

I left him the next morning and headed to my parents' house thirty miles away. I told them what had happened and how he had two more DUIs and how I didn't know what to do. I had just gotten married. I couldn't get divorced before the year was up! What was I going to do?

I had left Kevin before. I had left him a couple of times before we got married to reevaluate our relationship, to decide whether I wanted to soldier on.

Obviously, I returned to him. He was my drug, and I was addicted. Plus, I think deep down I thought he was my only chance to have a life—to have a family. I didn't think anyone else would want me. I settled for the drama and the alcoholism and the dysfunction. He was my life, and I would sacrifice myself for him. I was resigned, *but was I?*

When I had a quiet moment, my truth seeped through. I felt like I was behind bars screaming to be let out.

Get me out of here! This is the only life I get. I'm wasting it. I'm wasting my life. Let me out of here!

Oh, how I wish I had called the wedding off when I had a chance, but I didn't. And now I was stuck.

The next day, I went back.

Chapter 6

The Scapegoat Is Pregnant

Kevin was sentenced to sixty days in rehab for the third DUI and jail time for the fourth, not to mention fines and losing his license. The judge sent him to a rehab house where he could leave for his job during the day but had to report back to the house after work.

Rehab consisted of daily AA meetings and therapy sessions. Saturdays were family days when we all participated in classes and therapy. The classes taught us about addiction, where it comes from, and how it perpetuates through families and generations. I thought it was interesting to learn about family dynamics and where each of us fits into our families of origin and how it makes us who we are as adults.

One of those things that rang true for me and my family of origin was the concept of a scapegoat. The scapegoat is the one in the family who is selected to carry the burdens and problems of the family. This person becomes the target of abuse—a repository of all the blame or whatever, allowing the family to avoid dealing with any issues or finding solutions for family dysfunction. It was a relief to know there was a name for this drama that kept happening in my life. It wasn't just me. It was a thing.

I also learned a lot about addiction, about how the body is physically dependent on alcohol and how our minds are affected too. It gave me compassion for Kevin, which I hadn't had before. They mentioned codependency, but not extensively. I wish they had explained it more to the spouses. Maybe they did, and I didn't listen—or couldn't hear it—because I thought *he* had the problem that needed to be solved. I was codependent. That was why I chose an alcoholic—a partner with an equal level of dysfunction. Unfortunately, I didn't fully get that for another twenty years.

After the first thirty days, Kevin was allowed to come home for weekends. That was when we got pregnant. No, we weren't trying, but I think I kinda wanted to get pregnant, because I went off birth control pills when he went into rehab. I told myself it was to give my body a rest since I wasn't going to be having sex, but honestly, I didn't think about it. It was only two months. I was too scared or stupid to make an intentional decision, so I just let it happen. That way I wouldn't have to be an adult about it or ask Kevin and possibly get a no from him. I'm shaking my head even as I write this.

Kevin had been out of rehab for two weeks when I realized I hadn't had a period recently. I was at work when it hit me. I went to urgent care on my lunch hour and had a pregnancy test. In the waiting room, I had just convinced myself I was freaking out about nothing when I saw the nurse walking toward me.

I met her halfway and blurted, "It's negative, right?"

"Nope! It's positive!" she said with a smile.

"Really? Oh no! It's positive. Crap." I just stared at her, searching for another answer, I guess, or waiting for her to tell me what to do.

She didn't. She handed me my paperwork and told me to pay up front.

I left feeling excited and scared, but more excited. Kevin and I had the exact same brown hair, but our eyes were dramatically different. He had big blue eyes, and I had brown eyes. I knew from a young age I would have a daughter with blond hair and blue eyes. I don't know how I knew it, but I just knew this baby was *that* baby!

I never doubted for one minute of my pregnancy I was having a girl, and she was going to have blond hair and blue eyes. She was going to look like the perfect woman. She was going to have the beauty I always wanted—that my dad thought was beautiful. If I couldn't have it, my daughter would. And she did.

Wait. I'm getting ahead of myself.

Early in the pregnancy, Kevin had to go to jail every weekend for a month. In my la-la land, I believed he would straighten up after serving his jail time, and we would live happily ever after. I am again shaking my head at myself. But . . .

We moved into my brother's condominium, and my belly grew. The pregnancy went well. I wasn't sick. I told myself I was already fat enough, so I was determined not to gain weight. I gained two pounds. Kevin and I walked almost every day. It was the best thing I could have done for myself and the baby. I was in great shape when delivery time came, and I recovered quickly because of it.

Chapter 7

Codependent Much?

Kevin had no desire to move up in his job or to find another one, so I searched and found a better-paying position for him. I even submitted his résumé and would have done the interview if I could have. He got the job.

So halfway through the pregnancy, we moved to Elko, Nevada. I didn't want to work once I had the baby, and the only job I could find for him was in Elko.

Kevin worked with a man who was also from Utah, and he invited us over for dinner one evening to meet his family. Dillon and his wife, Millie, were high school sweethearts who got pregnant at fifteen and went on to have five children. Millie ended up being the only friend I ever made in Elko. I spent a lot of time at their house during the day because I didn't like being alone so much. We got along well and enjoyed each other's company. I liked their kids, especially the daughter. She was about eleven at the time, leaning into her teenage years.

One day, Kevin and I were at their house when Dillon got into it with his daughter, and she stormed off. I was about six months pregnant at this point, and I looked at Dillon with puppy-dog eyes.

"Awww . . ." I said, empathizing with both parties.

Dillon ran a hand across his face and groaned. "I hope you have a girl."

We laughed in the moment, but I never forgot that, because I was about to learn what it was like to have one.

I had started my prenatal care in Salt Lake City, so I wanted to keep my doctor and deliver with her. Dr. Macy, a tiny older woman, had been in the baby delivery business for thirty years. She was tough and no-nonsense, but not so much as to scare me. When I was thirty-eight weeks pregnant, she started having concerns about the baby's heart rate. She decided to induce me at forty weeks, exactly on my due date. Kevin flew in from Elko the day before I was going to be induced.

My labor was induced at 5:00 a.m. I labored all day long, with an epidural—thank you, God!

The doctor said things were going okay and that I could labor a bit longer. She encouraged me to hang in there and hustled away, her heels echoing off the cold hospital tile.

Kevin was in and out all day. Every time he came close to me, I took note of his smell. After living with an alcoholic as long as I had, I knew that odor. He seemed like Kevin all day until 6:00 p.m. From the moment he walked into the room, I could tell something was different. I smelled him when he sat down next to me, and when I questioned him, he didn't even try to lie.

"I just had a couple of beers. This is stressful!"

I couldn't believe what I was hearing. Had he really said that to me?

I had no words. I just turned my head and looked out the window at the falling snow. At that moment, my dad came in, talking about the storm and how it was the biggest one of the year. I was so relieved for the distraction.

At almost 10:00 p.m., my dad and I were chatting when I started to shake. He went white as a sheet and whispered something to the nurse. She immediately whisked him away.

A bunch of nurses replaced him, checking me, checking the monitor, telling me things. The doctor was on her way. How did I feel? Was I cold?

Time passed, and then I recognized the sound of Dr. Macy's heels on the tile as she approached my room. My thoughts had mostly been on myself and the baby until Dr. Macy walked into the room. She was all dressed up, like she had been at a party. Why was she . . .

My inner dialogue stopped. All eyes were on her. She looked at the monitor, grabbed the chart, barked directions to the nurse, then turned her attention to me.

"Michelle, we need to get that baby out of there. We are doing a C-section." She turned to the other medical personnel in the room. "Let's *move!*"

Right before the doctor started the procedure, Kevin moved in close to my face. "I love you, Michelle."

The force of his raw emotion was something I had never felt from him before. He had said those words to me, but not like this. It is a memory I hold close to me—the one and only time I saw this man be vulnerable.

I had noticed the clock when they wheeled me out of the delivery room. It was 9:50 p.m., and Naomi was born at ten o'clock on the snowiest day of the year in 1988.

They announced she was a girl. Of course, I already knew it. They bundled her up and showed her to me—she looked faintly blue. They whisked her off to the NICU. I later found out that her Apgar (the test which determines how well the baby tolerated the birth) was scored at 1. A normal score is 7 or higher.

Naomi had had the umbilical cord wrapped around her neck, body, and ankle. That was why she never dropped—she was tied up, literally. She had meconium in her lungs, which caused her to have pneumonia. She wasn't going home anytime soon.

Because of the C-section delivery, I would be in the hospital for a couple of days.

In the early hours of the morning, the nurse handed me my beautiful baby girl. I recognized her from my dreams.

"Hi! I know you."

I took her to my breast and fed her for the first time.

My life has begun.

Chapter 8

It's Not Just Me Anymore

I stayed with Kevin until Naomi was a year old. The baby didn't change anything. Life was filled with the same chaos we'd gone through for the previous four years. Him drinking, me catching him, him swearing he would stop, then stopping for a day or two. Wash, rinse, repeat.

I hardly remember much of that last year with Kevin because I worked the night shift at the casino and poured myself into Naomi during the day.

One morning, I returned from work at three, having left our baby in her father's care.

"Kevin?" I called out.

I entered the hall and noticed our bedroom door open and the light on. Reaching the doorway, I saw Kevin on the bed.

Why didn't he take his boots off?

I continued on to the baby's room, and the first thing I noticed was that the side of the crib was down. I hurried over to her. She was sleeping, fully clothed.

"Hi, baby." I gently put my hand on her chest, trying not to wake her. *She is soaking wet!* I patted her up and down. Even her hair was wet!

"Oh, baby, I'm so sorry." I gently removed her clothes and diaper. Her bright-blue eyes popped open, and the smile came when she saw me.

I cleaned her up, changed the sheets, got her in her jammies, and rocked her back to sleep. After I put her in her crib and put the side up, I let the anger come. It started slowly, like the heat of a fire when it just begins to burn, and then it dissipated. I stood in the doorway of our bedroom, watching him sleep. I took in the beer next to our bed, the smell his body emitted, and the fact that his boots were on. I shook my head.

What am I doing here?

Memories taunted me in a tragic sequence. All the times he'd let me down. The time he got drunk and embarrassed me in front of my friends or my family; the wedding breakfast; the reception; the wedding night; when we moved; when we met his boss and family for dinner; practically every holiday; when Naomi was born—what more did I need? *How much more, Michelle? How much more do you need until you are done with him, with this life?*

It was at that moment a thought came into my mind, loud and clear.

It's not just about me anymore.

Panic gripped me as I pictured Kevin leaving the stove on or a candle lit or the heater going, and passing out. We lived in a trailer. If there had been a fire, they would have both been consumed in minutes.

I can't stay. It's not just about me anymore.

Nevada is a remarkable state. You can get married on a whim, and you can get divorced the same way. I asked Kevin for a divorce on a Monday and filed on Tuesday, and we were officially divorced, signing papers on Friday. Kevin told me later he didn't think I was serious. He didn't think I would go through with it, but I took his yes and ran with it before he could change his mind.

Naomi and I left Elko and moved home to live with my parents. I got a job with the same company I had worked for before I moved, except in a different department. I would be processing medical claims for offices all over the country. It was a small office with about eight employees. I already knew half of them from when I had been there before, so it wasn't a hard transition. The job was perfect for a single mom—good hours, great benefits, and good pay with overtime opportunities.

We were going to be okay.

Chapter 9

Silver Fox Grampa

My parents were great. They were supportive, and they helped with Naomi every chance they had. My dad had retired, so he would get Naomi dressed in the morning, feed her breakfast, and take her to the babysitter every day I worked. I was very blessed to have their help.

I had been on the job for a week. One morning, I walked up the stairs from my parents' basement to see my dad—this big, burly, former marine—sitting on the barstool in the kitchen holding Naomi, his silver head bent over her in concern.

"She's not breathing right, Michelle." He looked scared—I'd never seen my dad look scared. "I think something's wrong with her. She's breathing too fast."

"Hi, baby." I searched her face and kissed her forehead to check for a fever.

She smiled up at me and jabbered something.

"When did you notice this, Dad?"

"This morning. I thought she was breathing too fast when I changed her diaper, but she seemed pretty happy, so I thought I must be imagining things. But after a while, I realized it was getting worse. She's struggling to breathe. Shouldn't we take her to the doctor?"

"Yes. I'll get dressed and call the doctor."

The doctor took five minutes with her and told us she had respiratory syncytial virus (RSV) and needed to be admitted to the hospital immediately. Since it was a virus, there was nothing they could do except give her oxygen and wait it out. They put her in an oxygen tent, where she remained for seven long days. I stayed with her as much as I could, but she would want me to hold her, and she needed to be under the tent so she could breathe—that was what the nurses told me. I would go home and worry, and then I'd go to the hospital and love on her, put her in the tent, go back home, wait, and then go back to the hospital. My mom went with me when she could, but my dad never came, until the fifth day.

My dad was as tough as they come, but he had a huge heart, especially for Naomi. I know he couldn't stand to see her in the hospital, but he finally made the trek. I'm thinking my mom probably talked him into it because she was awesome that way.

The minute he walked into the room, Naomi lunged out of my arms for him. He caught her and started to talk to her.

"Hi, Naomi! How are you? When are you coming home?"

She grabbed at his face and cooed at him.

"Well, I guess we all know who she misses the most!"

I complained. "She loves her grandpa!"

Everyone was looking at them when Naomi took her free hand and waved at the rest of us and said, "Bye-bye."

It was like she was saying, "Grandpa's breaking me outta this place! Later!"

Chapter 10

Missouri Bound, on a Mission from God

We moved out of my parents' house after four months and into an apartment. I found a babysitter named Sam, who used to be a nurse. She'd had to quit her job because she had lupus, and she couldn't keep up with the demands of nursing. She was a beautiful tall woman, with long, curly brown hair and an attitude that could rule an army. She was scary!

She was great with her son and Naomi, but she was tough on adults. I felt blessed to have her because she was willing to help me through that first year of being a single mom, but she didn't let me play the victim.

"Grow up! Be an adult!" She threw words like that my way when I started to whine.

Our work group was asked to go to Missouri to train another office to process their own medical claims using our technology and processes. I was eager to go, so I finished the lease on my apartment, moved home so my parents could take care of Naomi, and took off for the first two—of many—weeks in Missouri.

After six months of going back and forth, the manager of the Missouri office offered me a job—supervisor of training and auditing. It was a huge bump in pay and good benefits. I accepted the job, and on the day Desert Storm started, January 16, 1991, we got in my little car and started our trek across the country to Jefferson City, Missouri, to make a new life for ourselves.

I found an apartment and a daycare for Naomi immediately upon arrival. My parents had come with me, and they were generous enough to purchase furniture for us. I honestly don't know what I would have done without my parents' physical and monetary support during those post-marriage years. I often thank them in my mind when I see the struggles other single moms go through without support from their families. I was truly blessed that they were so willing to give.

The job didn't go as well as I had hoped. I was demoted. It was unfair. I was so humiliated and angry, I could barely hold my head up when I went in to work. I cried every night when I got home and sometimes during the day at my desk at work. I hated my life. I wanted to go home, but I couldn't bring myself to ask for more help from my parents, and I didn't have the money to move again so soon.

I looked for another job in Jefferson City, but nothing I found matched what I was making, even at my demoted position. I was also really good at my job, and with their incentive program, I could make a lot of extra money. I would do better to stay put. I felt stuck.

Soon after the demotion, I called my mom, crying.

"Michelle, come home. We'll pay for you to come home."

"I can't!" I cried. "God won't let me!"

There was something in me that told me I was right where I was supposed to be. I knew I couldn't walk away from this job—from this place. I just knew it. I didn't know a whole bunch about God, but I did know there was something more for me there in Jefferson City, and I had to stay to see what it was.

I made a good choice.

I knew I needed to make friends outside of work. I thought a church would be a good place to start, so when I saw a sign for Cornerstone Baptist Chapel in the parking lot of the daycare at the top of my street, I pulled into the parking lot and looked in the window from my car. I was about to pull away when someone in the building caught my eye. *Well, we have to go in now!*

Another good choice.

One morning, at three o'clock, I woke up with tears falling on my pillow. I sat up in my bed and cried out to God.

"I'm done feeling like this. I'm done hating my job and hating the people I work with. I can't live like this anymore. Please tell me what to do!"

After about . . . well, I don't know . . . a mind-numbing amount of weeping, a thought entered my mind, and the weeping stopped.

Go to work, smile, and stop pouting. I will take care

of the rest.

The next morning, I walked into the office with my head held high and a bounce in my step. I was actually glad to be there. When I passed my boss in the hall, I looked her square in the face and said, "Good morning!"

She nearly fell off her high heels. That felt good! I didn't want to be sad anymore; that wasn't me. I would be happy, loving, and considerate of those I worked with, even those who had treated me badly, because it didn't serve me to do otherwise. I processed medical claims for the next four years. God took care of it.

Chapter 11

God and Community

Church became my main social outlet. I was there every time the doors were opened—Sunday mornings, Sunday nights, Wednesday nights, and sometimes on Monday nights.

It was a small church with only about ten members, but it was growing. Some of the original members became good friends and helped me with Naomi. Ruby and her daughter, Julie, would babysit when I needed someone. Ruby became a mentor as well as a friend. She challenged me in my spiritual growth and encouraged me in my life. She was tough on me. She didn't put up with whining or victim behavior, which I was really good at.

I would get depressed and take on the world's problems—because we scapegoats become masters of scapegoating ourselves, even when there's no one to do it for us.

I would list everything that was wrong in my life and tick off all the bad decisions I'd made and whine about them. She wouldn't take it for long before she'd name off all the reasons I was blessed and all the people who were much worse off than I was. She often left me in tears, but I have to say, she was always right. So irritating.

One night after I'd put Naomi to bed, I was feeling sorry for myself and like I was never going to have another chance at being married and having a family. I called Ruby to get some encouragement. Don't ask me why I would call her. She was not the one to call for sympathy. Anyway, I went on and on about how it was so hard being a single mom and how I couldn't meet anyone decent, and even if I did meet someone, I could never trust them because all men were pigs.

Then I started complaining about money, and being a single mom is this, and being a single mom is that, and it's so hard, and no one understands, blah, blah, blah.

She probably listened for ten minutes before she said, "Michelle, you keep using the 'single mom' thing. I think you use it as a crutch."

I was blown away! How could she say that to me?

"What? What do you mean? *I am a single mom!*" I spat back at her.

"Yeah, I know you are, dear. I am a *married* mom, and I don't tell everyone I'm a *married* mom or a *remarried* mom. It doesn't define who I am," she said calmly.

I started to cry at this point and argued with her until she said, "Okay, Michelle, you take it to God. I'm just sayin' that you don't have to use it as a reason to be depressed. You have everything you need to live your life and take care of your daughter. You don't need to use it as an excuse as to why your life is hard. We all have hard lives."

I was thinking, *Sure. What the heck do you know, anyway? You just don't get it!*

But what I said was "Okay, you're right. I'll pray about it. Thanks for talking to me. Good night." I hung up, fuming.

Chapter 12

Complication

Kevin didn't have much to do with Naomi unless I made the connection happen. He was still living in Elko, so if I knew either of us was planning to be in Utah, I would make a point of getting them together. Kevin was not good at pursuing his daughter, and neither were his parents. They would all complain they didn't see her, but they seldom made the effort to make it happen.

When we had been in Jefferson City for almost a year, Kevin called and told me he wanted to see Naomi more often. He had begun to pay child support, so I thought this might be coming.

Kevin had married a woman named Kathy, and she was bound and determined to get Naomi for regular visitation. They hired a lawyer, and so did I, and we hashed it out. Naomi had to stay with them for eight weeks during the summer, plus every other holiday if they wanted to pay for it—which they didn't, so she only had to go for eight weeks in the summer.

She was only two years old the first time she went to her dad's house. She was leaving her mom for eight weeks, really the only consistent thing in her life. I'm sure that had to affect her somehow. They say kids are resilient. That was what I kept telling myself, but I wondered how her little brain processed being away for so long without her mom.

That time was the hardest on me. It was strange not having anyone else to think about or to care for. I spent a week feeling numb, before the reality of her being gone sank in. And when it did, it was like an avalanche.

I felt anxious and unsettled. Then the anger came. Then I started to mourn. I missed her little hand in mine and her sweet smile. The more I thought about her, the more I missed her, and the more I felt like I was going to die! My heart physically hurt, and I bawled until I couldn't breathe. I didn't know what to do with myself. *How am I supposed to live through the next seven weeks? Oh God! I can't take it!*

After a while—it seemed like a long while—I calmed down and realized I had to make it through. I had no choice. She was gone, and she wasn't coming back for seven more weeks. *I must get through these weeks without her.* So I got busy and distracted myself from the emptiness. I went dancing and to the movies, and I took my time at the gym. I pushed through until I got her back, which I finally did, safe and sound.

The second summer she went, Kathy and her sister picked her up, and they drove across the country. I can't remember where they were coming from, but they drove through Jefferson City and picked her up. I was going to my parents' house in ten weeks—yes, ten weeks this time, because of work constraints. My parents took her after the eight weeks, and she stayed with them until I could get there.

While she was still at her dad's, I called to talk to her. They put her on the phone, and we were talking about her day when I heard what sounded like the outside door close. I asked Naomi if anyone was there with her.

"No, Mom, I'm here all alone. I am a big girl!"

What is happening? She is three years old! She is not to be left alone!

"Um . . . Honey, what do you mean you are all alone? Where's your dad? Where's Kathy?" I tried to sound calm and collected because I definitely didn't feel anything close.

"They're gone, Momma! I'm home alone like a big girl!"

My mind was going ninety miles an hour. I tried to figure out a way to get to her, to make her safe. I could call my parents; they were four hours away. How about social services? But did I want to get them involved? Did I know anyone in Elko? Not anymore—it had been years, and people moved out of there so quickly. I'd had one friend, but I had lost touch with her. *Dear God, what am I going to do?*

In the midst of my frantic brainstorming, I heard the door open.

"Naomi, did someone come inside? Who came home?"

"Give me that phone!" I heard the irritated voice of a young male, who didn't sound familiar to me.

Naomi screamed for me as the phone slammed down. I hung up and called right back. No one answered.

Finally, after five hours, I got someone. It was Kathy.

I tried not to lose my temper. "Naomi was on the phone with me today when she was left home alone, and then someone ripped the phone out of her hand and hung up. What's the deal, Kathy? Why is she home alone? She's three years old!"

"Oh, Michelle, she's fine. We were just down the street. She knows where we go. It wasn't that big of a deal." Condescending and patronizing.

Meanwhile, I heard Naomi in the background screaming her head off. "Kathy, what's wrong with her? Why is she screaming? Can I talk to her, please?" I fought back the tears.

"Just a minute. She's mad because she had to take a bath." Kathy set the phone down. I could hear her talking to Kevin about me being irrational, and then Naomi came on the line.

"Hi, Momma," she said, catching her breath between sobs.

"Hey, baby. I love you. Are you okay?" I was dying. "Let me sing you a song, sweetheart."

I can't remember what song I sang—it was probably "Little Bunny Foo Foo" or "Do-Re-Mi." Her sobs slowed with each note. I told her to imagine me holding her and singing to her, especially when she missed me.

After the ten weeks, I flew to Utah to pick up Naomi. I couldn't wait to get my hands on that baby, to get her home, safe and sound.

I was supposed to get into Utah at 7:00 p.m., but my flight was delayed, so I wouldn't get there until three in the morning. I was so disappointed because I had been looking forward to having Naomi meet me at the airport.

I figured now she wouldn't, since it was so late. I called my parents to let them know of the delay.

"Hi, Mom! I'm not going to make it into Salt Lake until 3:00 a.m. I'm so sorry. I know it's late."

"Oh boy, okay. Naomi is so excited to see you. I hate to tell her you'll be late."

"I know. I'm sad too. Let me talk to her." I took a deep breath and swallowed back the tears.

"Okay, here she is." Then, to Naomi, she said, "Honey, this is your momma. She is going to be late. Her plane broke, and they have to fix it."

Naomi took the phone. "Hi, Momma!"

"Hi, baby! How are you?"

"Your plane break, Momma?" She sounded so worried.

"Yes, but they are fixing it, and I'll get there as soon as I can."

"Did all the air come out of it?"

Tears turned to laughter.

Finally, I made it to Salt Lake. I got off the plane, looking for someone I knew. I wasn't sure who was going to pick me up. I didn't see anyone familiar. I had started toward the pay phones when I heard "Momma!"

I turned around and saw my sweet baby running toward me at full speed. She was in a beautiful dress with her hair all done up. Everyone in the vicinity stopped and watched as this child and momma ran toward each other. I grabbed her in my arms and swung her around, not wanting to ever let her go again.

Thank you, Jesus!

When Naomi was five, I found out how hard things were for her at her dad's house. I'm not sure why she didn't tell me sooner. Maybe she was too young to tell me what was happening, not having the words to explain herself, or maybe it didn't cross her mind to tell me. It all came out on the Fourth of July while we were perched on a hill overlooking the Missouri River, waiting for the fireworks to start.

"I slept on the floor at Daddy's house." She scanned the skyline for the first firework.

"You slept on the floor? At your dad's? Why?" It took me a minute to gather my composure, to catch up with the conversation. *Where did this come from?* I took a breath and changed the tone of my voice. *Be calm.* "Um, Honey . . . why did you sleep on the floor?"

"Bobby." Her twenty-year-old stepbrother. "He came to my bed while I was sleeping and climbed in with me. There wasn't enough room, so he pushed me onto the floor."

"Why did he sleep in your room?"

"Don't know."

"I'm so sorry you had to sleep on the floor, Naomi. Did you tell your dad?"

"No, I just went to sleep and let him sleep on the bed. He was stinky, anyway." She wrinkled her nose and shook her head.

Thoughts penetrated my mind as I tried to work this new information out in my head. *Did he do anything inappropriate? Should I ask her? I don't want to put anything in her head that didn't happen, but I need to know if something happened. What should I do?*

Naomi broke the silence by asking me when the fireworks were going to start.

"Really soon, Honey. Just keep watching toward the river." Taking another breath, wanting to sound conversational and not angry, I continued. "Did Bobby hurt you, or make you feel scared at all?"

"No, Momma. He was smelly and pushed me out of bed."

What were they thinking, having a drunk twenty-something-year-old man bunk with a five-year-old? My stomach hurt.

"Momma, look!"

The fireworks had begun, which pulled me out of the anger of the past and into the present, where my baby's face was lighting up with each boom and spray of color.

Since Naomi had spent her last visit with her grandma, I realized this had to have happened when she was three or four. Whenever it happened, it broke my heart to think of the things that child endured when she was visiting her dad. I wished she were all mine and didn't have to go visit him and that awful woman he married. But she did, and there was nothing I could do to stop it.

Chapter 13

Naomi's Prayer

When Naomi was five, her summer visit was uneventful because she stayed with Kevin's parents, and Kevin visited her there. His living situation had changed dramatically since the year before because his wife had left him for another man and moved to California. Kevin was living in a house filled with men and didn't have room for Naomi, thank God. Kevin's parents were great with her, taking her to feed the ducks and teaching her how to tend a garden, and even nursing her through a bout of chicken pox.

One morning, after her return home from Utah, Naomi and I were making my bed.

"Momma, we need to pray for a husband for you and a daddy for me."

I was shocked at her request. I had thought she and I

were doing great together. I was offended that she felt like she was missing something. *You mean, I'm not enough?*

"Why, Honey?" Feeling hurt. "Don't you think we are doing fine on our own? I mean, don't you have everything you need?"

"We need to pray, Momma. We need a husband for you and a daddy for me," she repeated.

Your child is asking you to pray. The command was audible. *You need to pray.*

When I hear the still small voice, I try to obey it. So we sat down on the bed, and I started. "Dear God! *If it be your will*, please send a God-loving man into our lives." I patted Naomi on the leg and whispered, "Your turn."

"God, please send a husband for Momma and a daddy for me who loves you as much as we do. Amen."

That prayer was the beginning of a whole new chapter in our lives.

I started teaching in the women's prisons with an organization called Prison Fellowship. I would go into the prison three nights every other month and teach a seminar to women who were starting their prison stay. We talked about stress, authority, sex, forgiveness, and faith. I would teach the lesson, then the table facilitators would discuss the material with their table, answering the workbook questions. It was a rewarding ministry. The ladies were grateful to have someone care about them and spend time with them. I was humbled and grateful to participate.

Shortly after we prayed the "husband-daddy prayer," I asked one of the table facilitators, Janelle, if she would tell me when their next singles gathering would be held at their church. I went to a small church with no other single people. She said they had planned a barbecue at someone's house that following Saturday night, and she invited me!

Saturday night arrived. Janelle introduced us around the party and then left us on our own. Naomi, the only child at the party, ran around talking to everyone and getting as much attention as possible. I stepped out on the back porch to see the view and enjoy the sunset. I socialized for a bit, and then realized I should get Naomi home and to bed. I walked into the kitchen from the back porch, and the hostess of the party, Diana, stopped me.

"Michelle! I need you to meet your daughter's new friend, Lance. Lance, this is Michelle. Michelle, Lance."

Sitting on the bench behind the kitchen table were the two largest men I have ever seen—Ron, who had red hair, round pink cheeks, and an inviting smile, and Lance, who was tall, dark, and handsome, and currently acting as my daughter's human jungle gym. She was crawling all over him, hanging off his massive arms, and giggling like the little girl she was. Lance, Ron, and I greeted one another, and then I said we had to go.

Later that summer, I saw him at another church event where we all met at Dairy Queen. When Naomi saw him, she made a beeline to him and catapulted herself onto his big belly, expecting him to catch her—which he did.

This time we had a chance to visit and get to know each other a little. Ron was there too, and since he was so much more talkative and outgoing than Lance, we mostly heard from him. Between the two of us, Lance didn't get much of a word in. He was tracking the adult conversation but mostly dealing with the child. He was so gracious to give her his time, and she was captivated by him. I never saw Naomi give anyone the kind of attention she gave this man. She trusted him. It was remarkable.

I had previously met a woman named Janice through church. She was a single mom with a daughter, and she volunteered to take Naomi for me when I traveled out of town for Prison Fellowship. I knew her before I met Lance. I found out they were also friends.

One morning, Janice invited me and Naomi over to her house for homemade cinnamon rolls. We got to her house around nine and noticed two trucks parked in her driveway. When Janice answered the door, we saw she had guests. Ron and Lance were there too. She invited us in and explained that the boys were going on a vacation to Colorado, and they wanted to leave one of their trucks at her house while they were gone. That was why they were there. That, and to load up on cinnamon rolls!

We put our breakfast together in the kitchen and went to the living room to eat. Naomi sat by Lance, and Ron and I were talking, talking, talking, like we did every time all of us were together.

After eating, Naomi asked Lance if he would take her out to the backyard to see the dogs. Minutes went by, and then Lance poked his head back inside and said one of the dogs had gotten out and he and Naomi were going after him. The rest of us kept visiting until Janice suggested we go out front to wait for them to come back. We were standing on the porch when we saw Lance walking up the hill with Naomi on his shoulders, playing drums on his head, and the dog in his arms. I heard that still small voice. *This is the man you're going to marry.*

I didn't hesitate.

Okay, God, then if I'm going to marry this man, you make it happen. I am not going to pursue him. You do it!

Janice took pictures of them as they hiked toward us. She captured a monumental moment. She had no idea what she had documented—the answer to a prayer.

Janice had a big gathering at her house a month after that historic Saturday morning. She invited me and Naomi. I wondered if Lance would be there, because ever since the cinnamon roll day, I felt like he wanted to ask me out. I would expect it to be him calling when the phone rang, and I'd ask Janice about him when I saw her. He never called.

The party was already in full swing when we arrived. I noticed Lance sitting on the couch quietly chatting with those around him. I worked the room, talking with this person at the kitchen table, that person at the sink, the couple sitting at the fireplace. I noticed Lance watching me. Sometimes I would catch his eye and smile. Other times I saw him out of the corner of my eye. I later found out he was studying me, noting how I treated the people around me and the way they responded to me. He thought I was pretty, but more importantly, he was interested in what kind of person I was. That was why he was watching me.

After a while, I went to him and plopped down on the couch. "So! How was your trip to Colorado?"

He smiled at me. "It was good. Thanks for asking."

"Well, tell me about it!" I coaxed. "What part of Colorado did you go to? Did you go to Pike's Peak? Did you hit the ski resorts or go to Denver?"

He patiently waited for me to stop shooting questions and come up for air so he could answer. "Yes, we went to

Pike's Peak. It was beautiful. We went to Rocky Mountain National Park, where we pulled off the road halfway up to take pictures of the scenery. Ron held out a cracker to one of the birds, and it landed on his hand and ate the cracker."

"That's so cool!" I turned my body toward him. He had such a DJ voice. Deep and sexy! *Oh, oops. Concentrate on his story, Michelle!*

"Yes, it was," he continued. "It was so cool, we decided to take pictures of Ron feeding the birds, and then we switched so I could get pictures with the birds. I was feeding one bird when this hippy chick came over to us and started scolding us about feeding the birds." He started to laugh and shake his head. "She was so funny! She had this hairdo."

"What kind of hairdo? What was so funny?" *Inquiring minds wanna know!*

Chuckling, he explained. "Well, how can I . . . okay, she had about a hundred braids or ponytails sticking out all over her head. She really didn't have enough hair to do what she wanted to do. She started with the birds and went into a bunch of unrelated things that Ron and I didn't want to know."

"How'd you get away from her?"

"We just got into the truck and left. We tried to be kind, but she wouldn't stop talking!" Shaking his head, he added, "Her hair was just so funny!"

Once I'd landed on the couch next to Lance, I didn't move the rest of the night. We talked all about his trip and about how he got sick with bronchitis when he got back. I liked his deep brown eyes and kind manner.

Toward the end of the evening, as people were leaving

the party, I noticed that whenever I went up to a group of people to say goodbye, they would stop talking and just stand there and smile at me. When it happened one time I didn't mind, but when it happened multiple times, I started wondering what the heck was going on!

Finally, I overheard one of the older ladies say to Janice, "There's romance in the air. Can you feel it?" She gestured to the couch where Lance and I had been all night.

I smiled and walked on by, wondering if she was right. Was this the beginning of something? He hadn't asked for my number or anything. I told God I wasn't going to do anything, that He had to do it all, but maybe asking Lance over for dinner wouldn't hurt. I did have a problem with my computer that I could ask him to look at . . . okay, I could probably figure it out, but it would be a good excuse to get him to come over. I was going to ask him. It was dinner. It would be fun.

I asked, he accepted, and the date was set.

Chapter 14

The Courtship

I am not a domestic person—at all. I don't like to cook, clean, organize, decorate, plan, or shop. It's overwhelming to me, and any woman in the world who is good at these things or even attempts to do them every day has my respect. I marvel at the women I've had in my life who have been able to juggle all these things at the same time and do it well. I'm a tell-me-what-to-do-and-I'll-do-it type of person. I've had a housekeeper most of my adult life because I *love* a clean house, but I don't want to have to do it.

All this is to say, I actually cooked for him that night. We had chicken enchiladas. Naomi was thrilled that he was coming over to the house. I'm sure she thought it was a playdate for her, so she talked about showing him her toys and her room.

We lived in a small three-bedroom house that I had bought after being in Missouri for two years. It was my first big purchase in my adult life, and I had done it all by myself. It was a huge accomplishment for me. The house had a big backyard and a basement. Mom and Dad came out the summer after I bought it, and Dad painted all the walls. He was great like that. I loved my house. I was proud of my house. It made me feel grown up and responsible and like I was giving my daughter the best I could possibly give her.

Lance showed up in his work clothes, and he was nervous as all get-out! He was sweating profusely, and even though Naomi kept him occupied, I could tell he was uneasy about being alone with me.

After dinner, we put Naomi to bed. Then I took Lance to check out my computer. It was an easy fix, which I secretly knew, but I thanked him, and we settled in the living room to talk.

Lance was easy to talk to. He wasn't much of a talker himself, but he was a great listener. He was wise in his council, and I noticed he didn't assume things. For example, sometimes I get to talking really fast with my brain going ninety miles an hour, and I'll say things that are not true or complete. I noticed he wouldn't let those things pass. He would stop me, ask me to clarify, and then either agree with me or discuss it further.

I liked him. I liked that he would talk, that he had opinions, and that he loved God in a way that was real and strong and full of grace. He was also supportive of the ministry work I was doing.

One time, I mentioned how one of the ladies I was teaching in prison couldn't read the Bible because the print was too small. The next day, he called and asked to meet me before I went out to the prison for the second day of teaching. He said he had something for me. Yep, you guessed it! It was a large-print Bible! (I found out later I wasn't supposed to give gifts to the inmates, so that didn't happen again, but wasn't that sweet of him?)

Technically, our first date was in October, when he took me to Springfield, Missouri, to see Mark Lowry, a Christian comedian. Lance held my hand for the first time. It was fun. We talked and talked all the way down to Springfield and all the way home.

While we were driving back in the dark of night, something hit the truck window, shattering it. We think it was an owl. What else that big flies at night? It was crazy! Thank God that thing didn't come inside, because it would have ended up in my lap.

He dropped me off at my house in the wee hours of the morning. Since Naomi was spending the night with Janice, I had the house to myself.

Around nine in the morning, I heard someone at the door. Lance! He had come to pick me up for breakfast. How sweet. He had Ron's car because his truck was getting the windshield replaced.

Later, when I saw his truck all fixed up after our owl mishap, it felt bizarre, like it never happened, or like it had happened in a dream.

Our dating life was mostly with Naomi—at the house or meeting at restaurants for meals. We seldom went out alone. It was like we became a family way before we legally became a family.

Naomi asked me if she could call Lance "Daddy," but I told her she had to wait until we got married. I was surprised by Naomi's love for Lance, because other men hadn't seemed at all interesting to her. I didn't introduce her to many men, because one: there weren't that many, and two: I didn't want her getting attached to someone she wasn't going to see again. I didn't want to put her in the position of having another loss in her life.

The only date I had introduced her to was Mel, the only other man I had dated longer than a couple of weeks, but they didn't really connect. It wasn't like Mel didn't try. He didn't seem comfortable around her, and I think Naomi could tell. Her attraction to Lance was so evident, so tangible, so immediate. It was like she recognized him and knew he was the one. The one God was giving her to be her daddy. Miraculous.

Speaking of Mel, I met him at a singles retreat, and we dated for a little while. He was nice to me, brought me flowers and candy, and even took me to meet his parents.

He was so much like Lance, it was uncanny. They both were in IT, they both had brothers very close to their age, they were both raised Methodists. They were the same age, raised in small towns, and even went to the same college. Neither one of them had ever had a girlfriend, and neither had ever kissed a girl, because they were waiting for the girl they were going to marry.

Why didn't I marry Mel? I ended the relationship before it got serious because Ruby, my mentor, suggested I ask God to show me the stumbling blocks of continuing my relationship with him. God showed me, through a circumstance with Mel's car, how much of a worrywart Mel could be. I knew I couldn't marry a man like that because I was a worrier too. I needed someone who didn't worry, who could talk me down and help me find peace.

I'm so glad I listened to Ruby and waited for the right man. Sometimes I think we take the first thing offered instead of waiting for the right thing.

Naomi went to Kevin's parents' house for Christmas, so Lance and I went to St. Louis to visit his family. I had already met his parents when Naomi was with us, but I hadn't met his brothers. This would be my grand introduction to the whole family.

We took Naomi to the airport and waited until the plane flew away. Lance suggested we take the train into St. Louis and walk through Union Station, which was decorated for Christmas. It was fun taking the train, and Union Station was busy and beautiful.

We walked around awhile, and I noticed Lance was being quiet and weird. He was stopping in stores and looking at the clothes. They weren't his size, and all the presents were bought, so I didn't understand what the heck he was doing.

We made our way to a huge, extravagant Christmas tree in the mall. I got bored, so I went to the windowsill that looked out into the mall, jumped up on it, and sat down, waiting for him once again.

After about five minutes, Lance came up and stood in front of me. "I have two Christmas presents for you. Do you want one now?"

"Yeah, sure!" I smiled. "Who doesn't want a present?"

"Okay. Will you marry me?"

Stunned, I shouted, "*No way!*"

"Um . . . shall I wait for another answer?" he asked with a big smile.

"I mean, yes, I'll marry you!" I threw my arms around him and kissed him. "I had no idea! That's why you were being so weird . . . taking so long and shopping for things you didn't want! Now that makes sense!" I hugged him again.

"Yep . . . that's why I was so weird. I was trying to get up the nerve to ask you. I love you."

"I love you too."

We announced the engagement to his family at Christmas, and we called my parents to tell them the same day. Everyone was happy for us. I was a little nervous about Lance's parents being concerned about him marrying a woman who had been divorced and had a child, but it never came up. They were incredibly accepting of me and Naomi from the moment they met us. I felt very blessed.

A week later, we made our way back to St. Louis to pick Naomi up from the airport. I was wearing my engagement ring when we picked her up, but I didn't think she would notice.

We were about to take her to lunch and tell her about the engagement when she pointed at my finger. "What's that?"

"Oh! Um . . ." I stammered, looking at Lance for some help, but he was walking ahead looking for the correct baggage carousel. "It's an engagement ring. Lance and I are getting married!"

Her only reaction: "Can I call him Daddy *now*?"

I smiled. "Well, I guess you'll have to ask *him*."

Of course, he said yes. Her prayer was answered. God had given me a husband and her a daddy who loved Him as much as we did.

Chapter 15

Biggest Man in the Room

Somewhere between the engagement and the wedding, I realized I had some fat-prejudice, and being around Lance all the time made me see it and question how it would affect our relationship.

Lance was a big guy. He was the kind of big that would make people stop and stare and say things. I don't think we heard anything rude, because he was tall and quite imposing, so people wouldn't be direct in their insults, but we saw the snickering and sometimes the pointing. My family was extremely fat-phobic, mostly my dad and my maternal grandma, so I grew up with them criticizing fat people, which included me and my grandpa, as I've said.

Because of this constant barrage of criticism concerning my weight, I took on the belief that I was fat and that

I must be thin to be accepted. That belief sent me on a lifetime of food issues and diets and, subsequently, caused my own fat-prejudice, even though *I* was fat. I was unacceptable because I was fat, so other fat people were unacceptable too.

Lance being super-fat put me in a quandary. How could I love this man and spend my life with him when he was unacceptable? The dissonance was deafening. I would have to settle my mind around this issue somehow.

Not long after Lance and I started dating, my dad's brother died, and they had the funeral in their hometown, Crane, Missouri. It was a two-and-a-half-hour drive from Jefferson City, so Naomi and I went, and Lance offered to come along. The funeral would be an opportunity for him to meet my family. We arrived late at the mortuary, so I was in a tizzy. Naomi wore a beautiful dress with a watch-me-spin-around skirt. As we were leaving the truck, she put her knee in the skirt, moved forward, and *riiiipppppp*. The skirt tore from the bodice part of the dress right on the seam, but it wasn't that big of a tear.

"Naomi, you're fine. Come on, no one will notice."

"Nooooo!" She cried. "It's ripped! My dress is ripped!"

"Naomi, we don't have time for this. Let's go. The music has started. We gotta get in there." I growled, pulling her out of the truck.

In a gentle but authoritative tone, Lance drew me out of my frustration. He put his large, warm hand on my shoulder. "Michelle, you go on inside. I'll take care of Naomi and her dress."

I stopped pulling on Naomi, looked at him, and asked if he was sure. He was. I went inside.

I'm not sure how much time passed, but it wasn't that

long—maybe fifteen minutes—when I saw them come through the door, hand in hand, Naomi smiling.

Huh? I wonder how he did that? I motioned to them. *I don't see the rip. Where's the rip?*

It wasn't until after the funeral that I found out what happened. Lance had found some dental floss and a needle and sewed up her dress. He sewed her dress with dental floss. That feat made him very popular with my dad, who was the king of jimmy-riggin' stuff. He was super impressed with Lance, which made my heart happy.

Now back to the weight thing. My paternal grandma, Shorty, never said anything about my weight, but she was super critical. She would watch TV and have something negative to say about every single person. It was annoying. Anyway, I was worried about her saying something mean to Lance, and I was worried his feelings would be hurt.

I told this to my mentor, Mary Kay, another strong woman placed in my life, and her wise counsel was this: "You need to let people be responsible for their own relationships. Lance is a big boy; I'm sure he can handle your grandmother."

It was the most interesting thing because all Granny Shorty had to say about Lance were positive things. She kept saying what a good-lookin' young man he was, and how tall and well-mannered he was. I laughed the whole time because it was so opposite of what I had expected. Lance was a hit!

I eventually shared with Lance my issue with fat people and how I worried about people being mean to him and how I was embarrassed when people stared and snickered. He explained how he'd been the biggest person in the room for many years and that he was used to it. Early on in our relationship, I would notice how he was constantly saying hello to people. I never understood why, and then one day it dawned on me. They were staring at him, and instead of feeling offended and ashamed, he would smile and greet them. Oh, my heck! What a sweet man.

Chapter 16

A Husband for Me, a Daddy for Naomi

We married on May 6, 1995, at the First Assembly of God in Jefferson City, Missouri. Both of our families attended the wedding, even my sister-in-law who was seven months pregnant with her second baby. It meant a lot to me because it was my second wedding, and everyone came anyway. I felt treasured.

At the rehearsal dinner, our dads were sitting together, and Lance's dad said to mine, "Maybe Michelle can speed Lance up and get him moving a little quicker."

Dad replied, "And maybe Lance can slow her down a bit."

That's what couples do: even each other out. And that was exactly what we did.

The wedding was beautiful. Naomi was the flower girl,

and my nephew, Chris, was the ring bearer. Ruby sang with her quartet, and my longtime friend Shannon played the bells. I had a white wedding dress made for me. It fit perfectly. My dad walked me down the aisle to the wedding march and handed me over to Lance with a kiss at the end. It went exactly as I had hoped.

After the vows were said, before the God-joined-together-let-no-man-put-asunder, the pastor called Naomi up to the front and faced her toward Lance.

Lance pulled out a necklace from his tux pocket and put it around Naomi's neck. "Naomi, I am so happy to become part of your family. Here is a necklace to remind you I will always be here for you. I love you very much."

She rushed into his arms, and they hugged each other tight.

The audience's reaction was audible: tears, gasps, some with both. They had just witnessed the creation of a family, and it was good.

I had parented Naomi by myself for five years before Lance came into our lives. Sharing parenting responsibilities was difficult for me since I'd never had to do it. Lance jumped from being a single man to being a husband and a dad to a six-year-old girl. He was not great at communicating to others about what he was thinking, and that caused some problems early on, especially in the parenting realm.

This became very apparent one day when I was helping Naomi get dressed for school. I grabbed her new spandex pants her grandma had bought her and a tank top.

"Here. Put these on. They look cute together," I said, holding the outfit out to her.

Putting her hand up like a policeman stopping traffic,

she said, "No! Daddy said I cannot wear these pants any-more because they are in'ppropriate."

"What? He said what?" I scowled. "He didn't tell me anything about it!"

"Yep! Daddy says they are in'ppropriate. I can't wear them anymore, Momma."

"Okay!" I said, feeling so irritated. *Who does he think he is telling me what my child can and cannot wear? My mom bought those clothes for her! She is not going to be happy when Naomi doesn't wear them, and furthermore, where does he get off making a rule for her and not talking to me about it, or at the very least letting me know he made it?*

We picked something else for Naomi to wear and headed to the kitchen for breakfast. Naomi had gone on ahead of me, so when I entered, ready to pounce, Lance was standing near the sink, facing me, holding Naomi in his arms.

"What's the deal about Naomi not wearing spandex pants?" I growled. "You know my mom bought those for her. What's your problem with them?"

"I don't think tight pants are appropriate for a little girl to wear. Actually, I take that back. I don't think they are appropriate for *any* girl to wear. Too revealing," he explained.

"She's only six years old!" My voice rose. "It's not like anyone is going to look at a little girl's butt. I could un-derstand it if she was fifteen, but she's hardly got a butt!"

The anger built in me as I experienced this loss of total control in my daughter's life. I was so pleased to have a man in Naomi's life, to love her and nurture her, but I nev-er thought about the other side of another person's opinion in parenting her and that it might be contrary to my own. The more I struggled against relinquishing this control, the angrier I got, and before I knew it, I was stomping my feet like a little girl.

"Man! This is ridiculous!" I spat the words at him as my six-year-old watched.

"It's okay, Momma. I don't need to wear those pants," she said in her sweet voice. I'm sure she was wondering what was wrong with her otherwise happy momma.

"*Fine!*" I exclaimed. "Next time, could you please tell me the rule before you tell my child?"

"Yes, I sure will. I'm sorry I didn't tell you the rule before I made it. I will try and do better next time," he said.

"I'm going to work!" I shrieked as I stomped out of the room.

Chapter 17

Kevin's Last Act

We were married for six weeks when the call came. I had served the family dinner and was about to sit down. I picked up the phone. "Hello?"

"Uh, Michelle? This is Elsie."

Kevin's mom.

"Oh, hi! How are you?" I was thinking she was calling to talk to Naomi.

"Um, not so good. Kevin died last night." Her tone was flat, rehearsed.

"How? What? When . . ." I stammered.

"He shot himself." Blunt—she'd had to say these terrible words too many times already, poor thing.

I don't remember anything after that except telling Naomi. Mary Kay advised us not to tell her until we had everything planned so we could answer her questions intelligently. I didn't want to tell her at the house because you always remember the place where you hear bad news, and I didn't want her to associate her home with this. So I took her to my office when no one was there. I picked Naomi up and set her on the desk. Lance and I sat in front of her.

"Naomi, I have something very important to tell you."

"Okay, Momma." Mirroring my serious face.

"Honey, your dad died. Kevin died."

"How did he die?"

"He shot himself in the chest with a gun. We don't know what happened, if it was an accident or what. All we know is he died from shooting himself."

We were all silent for a bit, and then she did the most interesting thing. She smiled. Her reaction made me think she didn't understand what was going on.

"Naomi, your dad is dead. He's not coming back. Do you understand?" I searched her face for a hint of what she might be thinking.

She was still smiling. "Yeah, but I only have to love one daddy now!"

Wow. That was a glimpse into my little girl's mind. She was conflicted about loving Lance so much because she had an obligation toward her biological father. The burden was lifted for her when one of them was taken out of the picture. God bless her little heart.

We flew to Utah and stayed with my parents. The moment we walked into the mortuary, everyone started circling around Naomi and asking her questions. I could see the panic in her eyes when she grabbed Lance's pant leg and started climbing him. He caught her up into his arms. She immediately calmed down when she was held high above the crowd, safely in her daddy's arms. As she looked around, she noticed the open casket.

"Mom, is that Dad in that box over there?"

"Yes, it is. They call the box a casket. Do you want to get closer so you can see him better?"

She nodded, so we made our way to the casket. Lance held Naomi, and she looked at Kevin for a long time. Lance put her down, and we walked into the chapel.

While we were walking, Naomi looked up at me. "He was so young, right, Mom? He was too young, right?" she said, tears filling her eyes.

"Yes, baby, he was too young to die." I picked her up and hugged her. "I'm so sorry, sweetie."

She pulled back and looked into my eyes and said one more time, "I just think he was too young, Mom."

Yeah, I thought he was too.

I called the city and asked for a copy of Kevin's autopsy report. They sent it along with the police report. Kevin and Kathy, who had reunited, were living in California at the time this occurred. They had been at a bar, and Kathy started flirting with another man. Kevin got mad and stormed out of the bar and went home. Once he got there, he pulled out his .22 rifle and shot himself in the chest.

Here's the weird part. According to the police report, Kevin stood up, put the rifle back in the closet, and went to the bathroom. They found him on the bathroom floor. I really think he was just messing around with the gun, thinking he was pretending to shoot himself. You know, like, "I'll shoot myself. I'll show her!" And then he shot himself, but I don't think he knew he did it. I mean, who would put the gun away and go to the bathroom if you shot yourself and planned on dying? Wouldn't you just lie down on the bed and wait for death to come?

Anyway, my theory is that his blood alcohol was so high he didn't feel anything. He shot himself, and he didn't even feel it. The bullet hit four different organs before lodging in his pelvis.

On the night of the funeral, Naomi slept on the roll-away bed across the bedroom from where Lance and I slept.

We were about to fall off to sleep when Naomi chirped, "Grandma said I would go to the school down the street if I lived with her, so that's where I will go when you guys die."

Silence vibrated through the room as we felt the weight of her words. What was she saying? What this six-year-old meant was, "I expect you and Dad to die and leave me too."

"Honey, Dad and I don't plan on going anywhere any-time soon."

"Yeah! You're not getting rid of us that easy," Lance confirmed. "Now go to sleep. Love you, Naomi. Sleep well."

"Love you too, Daddy. Good night."

I echoed the sentiment and drifted into a sad and un-easy sleep.

Chapter 18

A Family Is Born

Not long after we returned home from Kevin's funeral, Naomi asked me if Lance could adopt her. I told her I would put in the paperwork and make it happen. It took about nine months for us to get a court date to make the adoption final. It happened to be the day before Valentine's Day 1996.

We woke up that morning excited to be a family. We got dressed up and went to breakfast at a restaurant in town to celebrate. After breakfast, we made our way to the courthouse.

In the parking lot, Naomi wriggled herself between us, taking our hands and smiling from ear to ear. We entered the courtroom and sat down, Naomi crawling on Lance's lap and taking it all in. The judge finished with the people before us and then turned his attention to our lawyer.

"This is the Rohlf family, Judge. Lance Richard Rohlf has petitioned the court to adopt Naomi Logan, a seven-year-old child. They are present in the courtroom." He motioned to where we were sitting. "Mr. Kevin Logan, Naomi's father, is deceased as of July 6, 1995."

"Thank you, Mr. Anderson," the judge said as he looked through the papers in front of him. Turning his attention our way, he continued. "Naomi, do you want to be adopted by this man? It seems to me you kind of like him." He smiled.

"Yes, I want Daddy to adopt me, please," she said, burying her head in Lance's shoulder, feigning shyness.

"Then let it be!" The judge commanded. "Let the record show Naomi Gail Logan will now be legally known as Naomi Gail Rohlf, her parents being Lance Richard Rohlf and Michelle Lyn Rohlf." He banged the gavel down, adding, "God bless you! Have a great life!"

"Thank you!" I squeaked through tears. We walked out of the courtroom as the newly formed Rohlf family, completely blessed and created by God.

Later that year, I got pregnant. The delivery experience was so much different from my previous one. My water broke sometime during the night, so we got ready, dropped Naomi off at our friend's house, and went to the hospital. Even though I had had a C-section the first time, I was going to try a vaginal birth this time.

I had been in labor for ten hours when the doctor came into my room to check me. I wasn't progressing very fast, so she decided to increase the anesthetic so I could sleep.

Everyone left the room except for one nurse. Lance noticed how low my blood pressure was getting, and when he asked the nurse if that was normal, she said it was, and it should bounce back up. She left the room.

My body felt heavy, as if it were dissolving into the bed. I heard Lance yelling to someone. "Come in here!" His voice got further and further away. "Her blood pressure is really low! It's not coming back up!"

My once-quiet room filled with a flurry of people. I felt drawn away from the room and the people as they became outlines and then just blurs of movement. I felt like I was floating, leaving the bed, leaving the room. The last thing I heard before I went out was feet running to my bedside and a loud masculine voice barking orders.

Then, *bing*! I was back!

Lance told me my blood pressure had just kept going down, down, down, until he was alarmed enough to call for help. He said it stopped somewhere around 60/40 before they adjusted something and made it go up again. Probably the closest I've ever come to dying.

I slept all night until 6:00 a.m., when they woke me up to start pushing. They woke Lance up from the chair next to my bed, and we welcomed Lilo Nicole Rohlf into this world thirty minutes later.

She was beautiful and healthy.

Chapter 19

Go West, Young Fam

Lance and I had wanted to move west ever since we met each other. We talked about moving to Colorado and Utah, mostly, but we would have taken anything with mountains. Phoenix, Arizona, was the first place to offer him a job, so we jumped on it, sold our house, and moved. Lance went ahead with our pets to find us a house to rent, while I stayed behind with the girls to sell the house and pack. It was an extremely stressful time in my life, and I never want to do it again! Having an infant while packing an entire house full of stuff to move across the country was not what I called fun. In addition, Naomi was struggling.

Naomi attended a small school that she loved, but within a week of Lance's departure, she stopped engaging at school. She would sit at her desk for hours and not do a thing. Having Lance gone and our family separated did not sit well with her. I tried to talk to her about it, explaining we would join him in Arizona. We called him every night before she went to bed to say good night, but nothing seemed to get her out of her funk. I tried to find out what was going on in that eight-year-old brain of hers, but she wouldn't or couldn't talk about it.

I wondered if she was processing Lance's absence through the lens of Kevin's death, or maybe, more likely, watching her mother walk away from her at age two, and three, and four, when I was the only constant thing in her life. Being so young, did she think she was just spending a night, but then as the nights went by and each week turned into another, did she think she wouldn't ever see me again? Her only reference was the time that went by without seeing her mother. I'm sure she wondered if she'd ever see her new daddy again.

This was the first indication we had that Naomi might have issues with abandonment, and justifiably. It still took years before it manifested itself clearly in her life.

Her teacher was understanding. Not knowing what to do for her, I just kept sending her to school and encouraging her to do her best. I don't know. It was such a big change in her behavior when Lance left. She totally shut down.

Two of my friends from church helped me pack and get ready for the moving truck. Without them I would have been a mess!

I was on my way to psychosis by the end of the packing day. The ladies were upstairs packing, and I was supposed to be downstairs packing. When they hadn't seen or heard from me in a good while, they started wondering where I was and came looking for me. They found me wandering around the garage mumbling to myself. I was so overwhelmed, I couldn't do any more. I was out of brain space. They gently steered me up the stairs, sat me down, and told me everything was going to be all right. Thank God for good friends!

The house Lance found for us was in a nice part of town in a beautiful neighborhood of mostly older people. There was a family across the street with twin girls Naomi's age. We weren't there more than a day when the girls and their mom came over to swim. The mom, Sunny, said she was in the middle of getting a divorce and would probably be moving. She was nice and personable—someone I could totally be friends with. She was my first official friend in this desert place, and the twins were Naomi's first friends.

We had all been together in that house for about a month when Lance came home from work a little early. Surprised to see him home, I joked, "Hi! What are you doin' home? Did you get fired?"

"Ah, yeah, well, they said they didn't need me anymore," he stammered.

I walked over to him, wrapped my arms around him, and mumbled in his chest, "Oh my heck, Lance. Are you okay?"

"Yeah, I'm okay." Smiling, he added, "I thought, well, most men would go to a bar and drink their sorrows away, but since I don't drink, what should I do? I considered going to a bar and eating pretzels or peanuts or whatever it is they have to munch on in bars, but then I realized I'd be better off just coming home to my wife and daughters."

I hugged him again and laughed at his thought process. He was so trustworthy, proving to me again, again, and again he was on my side.

"Good choice," I said. "I would hate to have to bail you out of jail for overeating the bar's pretzels or peanuts or whatever it is they munch on in bars."

It may sound strange or irrational or like we were in denial, but we weren't worried about his job or lack of job. We were confident he would find another one, so while he updated his résumé and emailed it out, I packed our bags, and we went to California. Yes, we did! We took advantage of the time off, believing Lance would have many job interviews lined up when he returned home, which he did.

One of the offers was a consultant job where he would travel 20 percent of the time. We figured we could handle that, but the job ended up having him travel more, like most of the time.

The company originally thought they could drum up more business in Arizona, and Lance could stay local, but it didn't end up that way. He was gone for two weeks at a time, home a week, and gone again for another two. It was getting extremely difficult for me and the girls to say goodbye to him so much, and the stress of being the only parent, along with the loneliness of few friends and no family, pulled at the fabric of our marriage.

After a year of this craziness, God gave Lance the job that he still has today. A headhunter called him out of the blue from the résumé he had sent out the year before. Lance interviewed the next day and got the job. The company was in Arizona, so there would be little travel, but that meant we would stay in the desert.

Summer in Arizona was so weird compared to anywhere I had lived before. I noticed our neighbors were up early—like *early* . . . like before six in the morning—to do their yard work or to grocery shop. I had never experienced the heat of an Arizona summer, so I didn't quite understand the early start of their days, but it didn't take long.

Our first year it got up to 111 degrees, with the average being 104 during the hottest month of July. I would sit in my cool house with my girls and watch as the temperature was still over 100 at 9:00 p.m.

It was hot, and yes, it was a dry hot, except for some of the time when it was a wet hot during monsoon season, and it was miserable! I found myself getting up and going out first thing in the morning to do the grocery shopping and to run any other errands that needed to be done. It is definitely a different culture in the desert. People stay inside during the summer and are outside during the winter.

I remember the first Christmas my parents spent with us. My dad just couldn't wrap his mind around how beautiful the weather was on December 25. It was in the sixties—T-shirt weather for sure, especially for us mountain people. The first couple of years we were there, we would hike on Thanksgiving morning while the turkey was cooking. The sky was blue, the air was crisp, and it was what most of us lived for while we endured the stifling heat of the summer.

Winter is on its way, I'd tell myself. *Just two more months, and we'll be happy we live here.*

The worst part of my first years in the desert was when it was October and still in the upper nineties. That would just tick me off! I loved fall in the mountains, and in Arizona there was no fall. Well, I guess technically, there was really no winter. Temperature-wise, if we were comparing it to the mountains, desert winter is really mountain fall or spring. Sixties during the day, forties at night. It took me years to accept where we were, but I eventually learned to lean into it and just go through my day, no matter how high the temperature got.

I blame the weather that I couldn't make friends as quickly as I had in past moves. I think I was just depressed when we moved there. I had a new baby, and I wasn't in a position to reach out to other women. Lance was gone all the time, and I was trying to keep it together at home. It was exhausting.

In September I joined a Bible study at church, and that was where I met my friend Carol.

Carol had recently moved to town with her husband and young daughter, and she was looking for friends. I have always admired Carol for her ability to make friends and to create community. It was fascinating to watch her. She was bold—another strong woman in my life.

The way she tells it, I stood up and said something in class one day, and she said to herself, "I want to be her friend!" So after class, she asked me to coffee.

A lifetime later, we are still friends. Her daughter was eight months older than my baby, Lilo, so we did life together. I have always loved doing things with others. I'm at my best when I have people to work alongside, so this was a fun time for me.

Carol was impulsive like me, so sometimes we'd wake up to a beautiful day and call the other one and say, "Let's go to the zoo! I'll be there to pick you up in thirty minutes."

We were a perfect match. We let each other parent the other's child without offense. In fact, I learned a lot from Carol about constructive discipline. I was clueless with my

Naomi, and I was clueless with Lilo until I lived life with Carol and saw how she calmly disciplined her daughter.

One time when Lilo was two, she and Ella were playing in our backyard in the sandbox. Carol and I were out there too, just enjoying the cool air. Must've been in the winter.

Anyway, the girls went inside, and we heard Lilo scream out like someone had stabbed her with a knife. She came running to me and told me how Ella got mad at her because she wouldn't give her the purple My Little Pony, and Ella yelled, "I hate you!"

Oh. My. Gosh. That just crushed Lilo. She was out of her mind with grief. Carol sat Ella down and talked to her about what the word "hate" means and how we don't hate our friends. We can be mad at them and hurt by them, but we don't hate them. We tease them about the My Little Pony incident to this day.

Naomi, unlike Lilo, had a hard time connecting with girls her age. She tried and tried to make friends at school, but they never seemed to work out. I would invite girls over, trying to make a connection for her, but a friendship didn't materialize.

Naomi was more comfortable with adults. She would want to hang out with the teacher at school and hang with the adults at home or with the younger kids. We put Naomi in different counseling settings from the time she was eight years old, giving her opportunities to work through her tumultuous early life: divorce, death of her dad, remarriage, new baby, all the moves.

She was a lovely child, extremely well liked by adults. She was accommodating and service minded. I must admit,

I let her serve me and my friends. She'd say she wanted to, that it made her happy and she liked serving. I realize now she was people-pleasing, and she thought serving others gave her value. I just didn't know then what I know now.

One day, she came home from school grouchy. She had homework to do, so I put her at the table and told her to get to it. Homework was always a struggle, but this evening it was explosive. I'd had enough of her, so I handed her over to Lance when he got home.

From the living room, I played with baby Lilo, watching from a distance and listening to their conversation. Lance asked her if she needed any help and if so, what he could do.

"What do you care? You wouldn't help me anyway!" she accused.

Whoa, baby! Where'd that come from? I nearly came out of my seat, but I stayed put, somehow knowing Lance had to handle this.

Keeping his composure, Lance said, "I'm always willing to help you, Naomi. Now, if there's nothing I can do for you, you need to get moving."

"I don't want to get moving! You are mean!" She pushed the book and paper away from herself and stood up so violently the chair fell over backward. "You don't love me! You hate me!" She crumpled to the floor, her body heaving with sobs.

It was killing me not to go in there and rescue her, to hold her and talk to her, but something kept me in place. I was not supposed to interfere. This was between Naomi and her dad.

Lance sat on the floor and gathered her in his arms. Holding her as she cried into his chest, he repeated over and over again, "I love you very much, Naomi. You are my daughter, and I love you, and I always will."

Finally, she looked at him. "Some kids at school said I wasn't really part of the family because I was adopted and that Lilo was the real daughter, and I wasn't your daughter." More tears.

Lance pulled her away from his chest.

"Look in my eyes, Naomi."

She reluctantly met his eyes.

"I love you. You are my daughter. Nothing and no one can ever take that away from us. I wanted you, I adopted you, and as far as I'm concerned, I have never, ever, considered you to be anything but my daughter. You are as much a part of this family as Lilo. We just didn't meet until you were a little older than a baby. That's the only difference between my two daughters—when we met."

Naomi threw her arms around his neck and hugged him tight. "I love you, Daddy! I love you so much!"

The next day I was driving Naomi to school, which was a great time to talk about what had happened with her dad the night before. I drove out of the neighborhood before I began.

"Naomi, I'm sorry you felt you didn't belong in our family. I thought that was kind of strange, since it's always been you and me, hasn't it? We started this family, and then we brought Lance in, and then we brought Lilo in, but it was always you and me, right? We were together first—we were the beginning. Remember? It's you and me against the world."

I looked at her and tried to read her expression.

She looked back at me. "That's true, Mom. It was us first."

I smiled as I watched the road, and then she stared out the side window and added, "I don't know. I guess I forgot. Those girls said I wasn't really a part of the family since Dad wasn't my *real* dad. I don't know why I believed them."

I stopped at the school to let her out, but first I grabbed her hand and looked straight into her eyes. "Naomi, you always belong! Always! You are just as much a part of this family as any of us, and we love you very much. Please don't ever forget that. God put this family together, and it is a good thing. You are loved. Please believe that, no matter what anyone else says."

I grabbed her, and we hugged for a long time.

Chapter 20

The Sound of Music and Other Complications

I sang with my girls from the moment they were conceived. I would sing to calm them down, to cheer them up, to make a long road trip fun. Naomi started singing along with me from the moment she could form words. Our favorite song to sing was "Little Bunny Foo Foo," which came along with actions. I'd have her sing the song to anyone who would listen because she was just so cute!

Back when we moved to Missouri, my parents drove with us. Naomi would take turns riding with each of us through the many states.

At the end of the second day, we were eating dinner in the hotel restaurant. The waitress asked where we were from.

My dad told her. "We drove from Utah. Today we covered Kansas singing 'Little Bunny Foo Foo' five hundred times!"

Hearing the name of the song, Naomi struck up yet another chorus, and we all laughed at her tenacity. It was those types of situations that made me think she might grow up to be a singer.

Naomi had started piano lessons with Shannon when she was five. I would often talk about getting Naomi into singing, so Shannon entered her into a music festival. She helped her learn the two songs she would need to sing for the festival, "A Spoonful of Sugar" and "Castle on a Cloud."

After months of practicing, it was time for the festival. Naomi got up in front of the judges and sang her little heart out.

One of the judges was so amazed at such a little body having the confidence to sing to strangers that she commented at the end of her performance, "Well, Honey, look at you! Do you like singing?"

"Yes." Naomi crossed her feet at the ankles, pulling down on her dress.

"Mom," the judge said, "you need to keep her singing. She is very good."

I was so proud! At this moment, all the synapses fired in my brain, and the pathways were set. *This is the thing! She has a talent, something we can build on. She is going to be everything I always wanted to be and never was.*

She received an Excellent rating on both songs.

She continued to sing, mostly in church, in the children's choir, or in musicals. When we moved to Missouri, she auditioned for a group that traveled in the city and sang at different events. She was the youngest member.

The church we started to attend in Arizona had a support group called Confident Kids, which was a ministry for kids who had gone through difficult circumstances. There was also a support group for the parents to give us tools for how to navigate through the emotions that might come up as our children attended the group.

It was there that we met Bambi, a voice teacher. I asked her if she could take Naomi as a student. She charged a dollar a minute, which was pricey, but we made it happen. Naomi stayed with that teacher for five years, and she excelled.

The first time I heard her sing after she'd been seeing Bambi for a while was something I'll never forget. She stood in front of me and sang "His Eye Is on the Sparrow." She sounded so beautiful. The high notes were strong, the low ones full bodied and pure. She seemed so confident! I was amazed. Impressed. Excited. She would be a star! I would do everything I could to encourage this talent of hers, no matter what it took. Wow!

One of the things Bambi told me to do to encourage Naomi's talent was to have her sing in front of as many people as possible. This started my dinner and entertainment parties. Anytime and every time we had a gathering, I had Naomi sing to our guests. I bragged about how good she was and all the things she was doing. I felt so proud of her! She was doing the things I had always wanted to do. I lived vicariously through her, and it was awesome—for me.

When Naomi was thirteen years old, I found a homeschool drama group for her to join. It was brand new and run by a young woman named Shelly, who had recently graduated from a nearby Christian college. We quickly became friends, and I ended up helping her organize and grow the theater company.

Naomi didn't get a part the first semester. She ended up helping with the backstage management, but the next semester was a musical, *The Sound of Music*, and I knew she'd get a part.

After the auditions, they posted the cast list, and sure enough, Naomi had been cast as Liesl in her first full-length musical. I was so excited for her. I knew she'd be great, and it encouraged me to see her involved in something with other kids.

Naomi still struggled with making friends and getting involved. In four years of school attendance, she never made one real friend. I'd hear her mention someone's name, and I would reach out to the child's mother and set up a playdate. I'd make a nice evening of food and fun, and that would last for a week or a month or two, and then nothing. If I asked her what happened with that friend, she'd tell me they weren't friends anymore or they liked so-and-so more than her.

By fifth grade, I couldn't stand it anymore. A month into the school year, as we were driving home, I asked her my daily question of who she played with.

"Mom, I just help Mrs. Adams in the classroom at recess and lunch."

"Why? Why don't you go outside and play with the kids?"

"Because they're mean to me, and I like Mrs. Adams. She likes me to help."

I was frustrated that she wasn't making friends. I didn't understand it. She was beautiful and talented, so why couldn't she make this work? Her school life was not fitting my agenda, and in my ongoing effort to get it right, I blurted without thinking, "Do you want to be home-schooled?"

"Yes! I do!"

So that was what we did. We started homeschooling.

Chapter 21

Double Loss

One morning as I started my normal routine, the house phone rang. It was my dad.

"Hi, Dad. How are you?" I said excitedly. My dad wasn't the one who typically called, so I was surprised to hear his voice.

"Michelle, I have something to tell you. Are you sitting down?"

I sat.

"Lisa killed herself this morning."

"What? How?" Tears.

"She hung herself."

Lisa and I had not been close, but she was the only sister-in-law I ever had. She was a very private person. She didn't share much about herself, and when she did, it was only the facts. I never felt like she was my friend, or even wanted to be, but we were comfortable with each other and accepted each other.

I respected Lisa's honesty. She'd never pretended to like me to get to my brother like so many before her had. I was Dick's sister, not her friend. It worked for us.

Lisa was a ballet dancer, and because of her, I was exposed to the art of ballet. She was amazing to watch, and I was awed and envious of her discipline and devotion. Dick and Lisa had been together for twenty-one years.

"Where's . . . how's Dick . . . the kids . . ." I croaked.

"They are on their way out here."

Dick lived about thirty miles away from our parents.

"The police won't let them in the house, so they are coming out here," he said calmly.

What do I do? I gotta go. I gotta tell Lance.

"Dad, I need to go. I have to make plans to get home. Have Dick call me when he gets there. Bye!"

Then I called Lance, who was on the road heading for work.

"Hello!" he answered.

"Lisa hung herself," I cried.

"I'm on my way home. I'm turning around right now!"

I need help . . . I need help with the kids. What am I going to tell them? I called my neighbor across the street.

"Hello?"

"Alma, Lisa, um, I . . ." I was crying so hard, I couldn't talk.

"I'll be right there."

Alma was at my doorstep in seconds flat. She took the girls for a walk and then to Jamba Juice. Lance got home and called our pastor, who came over to help us make plans to get home.

Then Dick called.

"I am so sorry, Dick, I am so sorry." We both cried.

"What happened?"

"Bonnie woke up this morning and found her."

Oh, that poor baby. She's only four.

"Chris heard Bonnie screaming. He found her standing in front of Lisa's body. Chris cut Lisa down and called me. I didn't answer the phone because I was in the shower, so he called 911." Dick was in shock as he ticked off the events of that morning.

Chris was eleven.

How could this be happening? Oh, those poor children. How will they ever get over this?

"Oh, Dick, I'm so sorry," I sobbed.

"I moved out last week." Dick faltered. "We were trying to work things out . . . we had a fight . . ."

"Dick, it's not your fault. It's not your fault—she made the decision."

Silence, more crying.

"Michelle, Mom wants to talk to you."

"'Kay. I love you, Dick. We are on our way."

Mom got on the phone. "Michelle, your dad is having severe back pain. He's rolling around on the bedroom floor, he's hurting so bad."

My dad, as an ex-marine, had an ingrained tolerance for pain. He often told the story of the time he had his head stitched up without anesthesia. For him to complain, let alone show his discomfort, was completely out of character. I told her to get him to a hospital ASAP, and returned to my preparations to go home.

I was so far away. Everything was falling apart at home, and I was not there. I couldn't comfort anyone, help anyone. I had to get there.

Alma returned with the kids and sat down with me at the kitchen table. I had no news about my dad, so I called home. Someone answered the phone—Dad was at the hospital, and so was Mom. I called the hospital and found Mom.

"Mom! What's going on? How's Dad?"

"I don't know, Michelle. They are working on him." She seemed distracted.

"Mom! What do you mean, they are working on him?" I yelled into the phone.

"They are doing CPR."

Shock. Numbness. Denial.

I asked her to keep me posted and hung up the phone. Alma searched my face for answers.

"She said they are working on him." Hopelessness filled my bones. I felt myself lose control. "This can't happen! Two people don't die in the same family on the same morning of different things! I've never heard of it happening, so it can't happen. Things like that don't happen, especially to us. Not to our family. It is going to be all right. Dad is going to be okay."

Peace enveloped me like a hug. I calmed. "He's going to be okay," I told Alma. "God won't take both of them in the same morning."

Twenty minutes passed. No word. I called the hospital to talk to my mom.

"Hi. May I talk to Sandra Rickman, please? She's in the emergency room waiting area." I listened while the person on the other end explained where my mom was, and hung up.

Staring at the phone in my hand, I said to Alma, "They . . . um, they said my mom and Dick went home. I'm going to call my brother."

I reached him on his cell in the car. "Dick, what happened? Why are you going home?" My voice trembled, dreading the answer I already knew.

Dick's mechanical voice: "Michelle. Dad is dead."

The realization crashed over me—assaulted every part of me. Somewhere far away, I heard Alma yell Lance's name. Then somehow my husband was in the chair Alma had been in. I catapulted at him, screaming, wailing, sobbing. I felt the girls next to me on Lance's chest, joining me in the choir of grief and disbelief.

Not my dad! I just talked to him! This cannot be true! How could this happen?

We called the airline and got tickets. We packed and drove to the airport. Our flight was delayed, so we went to dinner. On the way back to the gate, I wandered away from the family, dazed. Lance ran after me and pulled me in the right direction. Friends kept calling, and I kept telling the story over and over again. This couldn't be happening.

The airplane was crowded, dark, and quiet. My family slept, along with all the other passengers. I fell asleep for a moment or maybe longer—I'm not sure. But when I looked out the window and saw the lights of Salt Lake City, the gravity of what I was going home to hit me like a pail of ice-cold water. I was going home to bury my dad and my sister-in-law.

My mother and my brother lost their spouses on the same day, on the same morning. I had to take care of them, be mature, and take control. I needed to plan two funerals. *Oh God, please help me.* How could this be happening? These things didn't happen to us! Not to me, not to my family. Tears fell as panic threatened to overcome me. The airplane was so quiet. How could all these people be sleeping when my life would never be the same again? *Oh God, please help me.*

At that moment, I heard God whisper to my spirit: *I will get you through this, Michelle. Rest, and I will get you through.*

We arrived at the Salt Lake City airport at 3:00 a.m. We rented a car and went to my childhood home, where Mom met us at the door in her housecoat. It felt like a routine visit, but it wasn't. We took turns hugging her, tearless, then picked up our luggage, and went to bed.

It was 10:00 a.m. when I ascended the stairs from the basement, the light bullying its way into my eyes, waking me up to the reality of this day. Neighbors were over, talking with my mom, giving her their condolences and, subsequently, to me too.

I heard Mom say she needed to be at the mortuary at eleven, but she was still in her robe, and the well-meaning neighbors seemed clueless. I realized I would have to keep on top of things. She was too overwhelmed to take care of herself, let alone everything else that was going on. My mom was independent and capable, but this was just too much. I needed to step in. I had to take the lead, so I did.

"Mom, aren't we supposed to be at the mortuary at eleven?"

"Oh, yeah!" She exclaimed, glancing at the clock. "I . . . um . . ." She looked at her helpless, clueless friends.

"It's okay, Mom," I said. "You go get dressed, and I'll say goodbye."

She waved an apology at the visitors as she hustled to her bedroom.

On our way to the mortuary, I found out Dick and the kids were staying with friends. One of Lisa's friends from Ballet West was taking care of her funeral. Thank God, I didn't have to plan two funerals—just the one.

The mortuary visit was straightforward. I asked to see my dad's body, but the mortician said he would have to get him ready, and I decided I'd rather remember him the way I had last seen him, when we said goodbye after our last visit just six weeks earlier.

Chapter 22

...Six Weeks Earlier

$\mathcal{D}$ick had left Lisa after months of trying to work things out. He was having an affair with another woman, and he decided he needed space. We had a trip planned to visit my parents and let the kids play in the snow, so we were there during this stressful time. I felt angry at my brother, and I didn't hide my feelings. Dick and Lisa had just finished remodeling their house, and Dick wanted us to come over for dinner so we could see it, but since he wasn't living there anymore, it was awkward.

We arrived around six thirty in the evening. Lisa was still at the house, waiting for some friends to pick her up. We all sat down to eat, and Lisa just stood there, waiting at the top of the stairs for her ride.

I felt so uncomfortable and angry. I wanted to scream at everyone at the table, "She is part of our family! What is she doing standing over there like an outsider? This isn't right!"

I was so mad at Dick for putting her in this position. I could only imagine how she felt or what she was thinking. Even though she was behaving like everything was fine, I knew she had to be dying inside.

As soon as she was out the door, I turned on my brother. "Dick, what are you doing? You cannot expect Lisa to compete with new love. Of *course* it's going to be more exciting than someone you've been with for twenty years."

"I know." He pushed his food around his plate. "But you don't know, Michelle. I have not been happy for a while . . ."

"Yeah, but that's no reason to go find someone else. You finish with one person and then start with someone new. You don't cheat!"

"It just happened. I didn't mean . . ." Dick tried.

"Oh, right! You just happened to have sex with someone who is not your wife!"

It went downhill from there. I kept confronting him, and my mom and dad—who hated confrontation—just stared at me. They'd never seen me stand up for something so vehemently.

I couldn't stop interrogating him until my husband finally stopped me. Lance didn't say much, and he seldom shushed me, but he did this time.

"Michelle, that's enough."

I stopped badgering. The table fell into small talk intermixed with periods of weighted silence.

We finished eating, cleaned up, and chatted about superficial things like the renovation, jobs, and the weather. Finally, it was time to go home. Thank God!

My parents pulled out of the driveway while my family climbed into the truck. Dick and I stood on the front porch saying our goodbyes.

I hugged him and said into his ear, "Dick, I just don't want you to end up a lonely old man."

Pulling away from me, he smiled. "Oh, Michelle, I'll never be alone. I'm too charming."

I rolled my eyes, punched him in the shoulder, and said, "I love you, Brother. Thanks for dinner."

The next day, my parents took the grandkids and us to a farm in the mountains where they rescued elk. Lisa came along too. On the way home, Dad and I got into a theological discussion about salvation. He had read the Bible more times than I had, but he still couldn't get his head around "faith" and, most importantly, God's grace.

"So! You are telling me if Jeffrey Dahmer accepts Jesus as his Savior in prison after all the horrible things he's done, he will still go to heaven?" he said.

"Yes, Dad. That's the beauty of salvation! It has nothing to do with what we do for God. It's all about what Jesus did *for us*. We can't work ourselves into heaven. If we could, we wouldn't need a Savior, now would we?" I loved talking to my dad. He was so smart, and it was fun to know something he didn't.

"Well, I don't believe it. I mean, what would be the point of being a good person if I could kill those who irritate me and still make it into heaven?" he argued.

"Yeah, I know, Dad. It doesn't seem fair, but God tells us that His thoughts are above our thoughts, and His ways are above our ways. Only He can know the hearts of men. I suppose He knows who is truly repentant and who is not." I was having so much fun!

That conversation will forever be imprinted on my

mind. I loved it when we talked. When I was little, he explained how Santa Claus could make it around the world in one night using a matchbook and a penny. He talked about how the time changes as the earth rotates. My dad was a very smart man. He just didn't believe it.

When people would say how smart he was, like when he'd answer every question on *Jeopardy*, he'd say, "Yeah, well, I'm a reservoir of useless information." My dad remembered everything he ever heard.

That evening, we were all sitting in the living room watching TV, something my parents did every night of their lives. I sat on the orange chair across the room, watching them as they watched the television. My dad was a couple of feet away from my mom, and Naomi was lying in between them with her head on my dad's lap and her feet on my mom. They were enjoying their granddaughter.

My oldest cousin once told me how the wrongs your parents did to you are all forgiven when you see them love your kids—their grandkids. There's a healing that happens, and I believe that is true. I would never have lain between my parents like that, but my baby could. It made my heart overflow with love for those parents of mine. It is a precious memory, one I will never forget, and the one I have burned in my brain as the last time I saw my dad's face. I will forever cherish that time.

Chapter 23

Two Funerals

We had two funerals that week, one on Thursday and one on Saturday. Lisa's was going to be first, at a theater in downtown Salt Lake City. Dick asked me to pick the kids up and take them to the funeral, but first I needed to take Chris to buy some clothes—some funeral clothes— to wear to his mother's funeral . . . oh God, help me.

I took him to Old Navy and waited as he tried some things on. I didn't know what to say to him, so we just chatted about things you chat about with an eleven-year-old boy. I kept thinking how normal he seemed, considering all he had been through that week. No emotion, not even shock—just Chris. I did try to get him to talk to me about what had happened at one point, but he clearly was not ready to put words to the experience.

It went something like this.

"Chris, do you want to tell me what happened that morning with your mom?"

"I just woke up and heard Bonnie crying. I called my dad, and he didn't answer, so I called the police," he reported.

I knew I shouldn't push any more. I would leave that up to the therapists. I was afraid of how I'd handle things if he did burst out with all he felt at that time. Would I say the right things? I didn't want to do any more damage than had already been done, so I let it go.

I think I might have said something like, "I am so sorry this has happened to you and your family. Please know you can talk to me anytime. I am always here for you."

Back to small talk.

We got home, changed for the funeral, grabbed Bonnie, and headed to the theater. Lisa's funeral was put together by one of her longtime Ballet West dancer friends. She did a fantastic job, totally honoring Lisa and her passion for ballet. Her funeral was like a performance. The pianist was from the Salt Lake City Symphony, and the speakers were from Ballet West. A video of Lisa dancing was projected on the screen as they talked about her accomplishments as a dancer and a mom. Her friend who put the funeral together talked about how graceful Lisa was in her everyday movements and how she could make something as routine as setting the table elegant—a performance worthy of paid admission.

The audience was filled with people from Ballet West and students from the university where she had been teaching dance. It was a lovely funeral, totally different from anything I had experienced before. Not a lot of tears or emotion, but it honored her life. It was a perfect end-of-life celebration for her. Afterward, out in the foyer, there was a spread of fancy finger foods like tarts and special cookies.

Funeral number one . . . check.

Dick asked my family to stay with them for their first night back in the house since that awful morning. He thought having us there would be a good distraction for the kids. When I got to the house and started up those stairs, I stopped at the landing, letting it sink in that this was where Lisa had taken her last breath. I was so sad for her, for the kids, for my brother. Suicide is such a permanent decision, one that affects all those who are left behind for the rest of their lives.

We were not strangers to suicide. My uncle, my dad's brother, killed himself when he was in his thirties. He called my dad the night before he did it, and my dad was never the same. He sank into a depression that lasted for a long time, and even after that, he couldn't talk about his brother without getting teary.

After dinner, Lance, Dick, and I were sitting on the couch talking. We started talking about God things for some reason, and Dick said God would never want him after everything he'd done. He even wondered if he was being punished because of the way he lived his life.

"I don't think God works that way, Dick," I said. "Do you, Lance? Do you think He gets back at us?"

"No, I don't think so." Then he added, "God already knows everything we will ever do. It's not like He's keeping cosmic score on everyone, making decisions about our lives by the choices we make. His ways are so much bigger than playing the tit-for-tat game we humans play with one another."

"Well, I don't need it. I don't need religion. I'm way past all that stuff," Dick said.

"Just know, Dick," I said gently, "if you ever need someone, God is always there for you. He loves you, no matter what you have done. We are all sinners, and He loves us anyway."

I could tell the conversation was over by the glaze that descended over Dick's eyes, so I dropped it. It was time for bed.

On Friday, it was time for *me* to go shopping for funeral clothes. Lance and I went to the local mall and were in the women's department when Lance got a call. It was his mom.

"Hi, Mom . . . oh, right! Thank you."

What is going on? What are they talking about?

Chuckling, Lance said, "Yeah, I guess I didn't realize what day it was, or the date."

And then it dawned on me. It was March 10, Lance's birthday, and not one of us noticed—not even Lance. I felt bad I hadn't remembered his birthday, and even worse that he hadn't either.

I was shaken by it—the gravity of the situation confronted me once again. We were in a vortex, in a place where few people go . . . and a place where time stops and survival is all there is. Real life, normal life had been put on hold so we could attend to the surreal, the interruption of life: the reality of suicide, death, loss, and the ending of life as we'd always known it. This week would change me forever.

Dad's funeral was at the local mortuary. My parents had bought one of those insurance policies where you pay for your funeral before you die, so we didn't have a lot of decisions to make—they were made.

Lance and I arrived a little late and knew there would already be people milling around, waiting for it to start. I was a robot at this point. I needed to get through this funeral. It was the last one of the week, and I just needed to soldier through. I was all cried out—didn't have anything left.

Yeah, well, that was what I thought. We walked through the doors of the building, and the first people I saw were two friends of mine from high school. They loved my parents and spent substantial amounts of time with my family. I hadn't seen them in twenty years, and when I saw them walking toward me, I burst into tears.

We embraced each other, and through the tears I mumbled, "I can't believe you're here . . . oh my gosh, I can't believe you came."

In one moment, I was a teenager again, hanging out with these beautiful friends and feeling like I was home at my house, happy, without a care in the world. I leaned into it, trying desperately to hang on to the memory, to the simple days.

But it wouldn't last, it couldn't last—it was only a memory. I was ripped away from the comfort of the past by the treacherous, unyielding present. It was time to go into the service. The funeral had begun.

The chapel was small and bursting with people. Once the chairs filled up, people lined the walls and stood in the back. My childhood friend Mary played the piano while I sang "Amazing Grace." A family friend officiated the service. People were given the opportunity to share a memory of my dad. My friend Chad, whom I grew up with and who was at every significant event in my life, was the first to speak.

"Mr. Rickman would buy Halloween Spook Insurance from me when I sold it for the Boy Scouts, and after I turned twenty-one, he'd offer me a beer every time I walked through his door. I will always remember him as a big part of my childhood. He was a good man."

The next person to stand up was my friend Mary. She talked about waking up at my house after a sleepover and my dad cooking chocolate-chip pancakes.

Then, Bill Smith, a son of my parents' friends, stood up and told the story of when my dad came to his rescue.

"I showed up on Rick's doorstep one evening with a broken arm. My dad was gone on deployment, so it was natural for me to go to Rick's for help. Rick looked at my arm and took me to the emergency room. He was always the one I'd go to—that all of us would go to. Thank you, Rick. You'll be missed!"

Person after person talked about the things my dad did for them, his love for football and many other things, but mostly, they talked about how he could tell a story and how he loved to make you laugh. He was good at making people laugh. It was a great service, one full of love and memories of a life well lived.

Funeral two . . . check.

I stayed for two more weeks with my mom to make sure she was okay, and then we went back to Arizona.

Chapter 24

Processing

I went to the doctor shortly after returning home. I was put into the examination room, and the nurse started asking me questions about my health.

"Are both your parents living?" she asked.

"Yep!" I said, and then I looked at her and burst into tears. I tried to tell her I had just got back from burying my dad, but I couldn't even talk.

Finally, I was able to get ahold of myself enough to tell her my dad was no longer living. That was crazy. It was like my brain still didn't believe my dad was gone. I guess that's what they call "denial" in the grieving world. Funny how we don't march straight through the stages but instead wash back and forth through them, like the waves on the shore.

When I first got home, I didn't know what to do with

myself. I felt so lost. I would find myself wandering around the house in silence, just clueless about what to do next.

One day I got a phone call from a lady I had met briefly the week before my dad died. She told me I had been on her mind since she'd heard about my dad and sister-in-law. She had been praying for me and wanted to know if I wanted to meet with her and talk about what I'd been through.

I hadn't had a second to process all I had experienced during those three weeks in Utah. I hadn't processed the funerals or the events leading up to the funerals. I had spent those last three weeks meeting other people's needs—my kids, Dick's kids, Dick, Mom. I was so focused on everyone else, I didn't take the time to listen to what I needed or what I was thinking or feeling.

It was only after I got home that the small pieces of ice started to let loose, warning of the avalanche to come. The feelings I'd had since I got home were swirling around in such a way that I didn't even know what I was feeling. There was the sadness of losing my dad, the anger toward Lisa for what she had done to her kids, and then there was Dick. I was angry at him for not being there, for leaving his kids, for leaving Lisa, for being drunk. But then tears would flow when I'd think of my niece and nephew growing up without a mom and—if Dick didn't get it together— without a coherent dad.

This call felt like a lifeline, a chance to excavate all those feelings I'd been holding on to. Maybe this would be a safe place to look at them, to let them go, to move through the grief, to live.

I was silent for a second, staring at nothing, trying to think of a reason not to say yes, and I couldn't think of a thing. I was lost, and I believe God had sent me yet another strong woman. God keeps sending me women who have been through their storms and have come out the other side, stronger and better. There's a message in this for me.

"Okay, yeah, sure. Thanks, that sounds good." I hung up and cried.

Chapter 25

Another One

My brother called in the fall of 2005, five years after losing Dad and Lisa.

He caught Naomi and me driving home from the airport, returning from our trip to Europe. We had planned, worked, and saved for the trip to Germany, Switzerland, and Austria in celebration of Naomi's sixteenth birthday.

"Hi! We are just getting home from Europe! What's up?"

"Ah, well, I guess I'll just say it. Mom has lung cancer," he blurted.

Well, that was the beginning of a long eight months.

I got home, talked to Lance, washed laundry, repacked, loaded the girls, and headed for Utah. My mom had been in Hawaii when Dick opened the report from the hospital. He took it to a pulmonologist friend of his and asked him to interpret the lung x-ray. Dick said the doctor asked where my mom was right then, and when Dick told him, he said that it was a great place to be, because it didn't look good.

We were sitting on her couch after she was diagnosed.

"I knew I was going to die, Michelle. I told Lucy when we were in Hawaii how I had a feeling I was going to die soon."

"How did you know, Mom? Was it because you got that lung x-ray and knew it wouldn't be good?"

"Yeah, no . . . I don't know. I had a feeling I needed to get an x-ray, and since the hospital requires one a year in order to volunteer there, I went in and had it done for this year. I didn't feel bad—I just had a feeling."

She had stayed with us earlier that year, and one morning she woke up with a pain in her right arm. She said it was a weird pain, and when I asked her if she remembered doing anything to it, she didn't. The lung cancer was in her right lung. I wonder now if that was the beginning of the cancer. She never complained about her right arm hurting again, but I'll always remember that day. You know, the whole "what if" game we play with ourselves.

Well, she was right. She was on her way out.

I spent as much time as I could at my mom's house, taking her to doctor appointments and trying to be with her as much as possible before she got too sick to do anything. Sometimes my kids were with me, and sometimes they stayed home.

During Christmas, we had a "Celebrate Sandra" party. I invited all her friends, explaining to those who didn't know about the cancer how we wanted this to be a fun time for her to see her friends and for her friends to see her.

The party was well attended. Mom sat in her recliner and visited. They reminisced about the last forty-two years living in that house. Years of raising kids, parties, graduations, and funerals. They talked about my dad and football and beer. It wasn't sad at all.

Okay, it was a little sad for me, especially when I talked with someone about the reality of the situation. That was when the tears came.

Many of the guests were in denial and asked me if it was true, if there really was no hope, nothing left to do. Other than those private times, everyone kept a happy face for my mom. I was thankful for those smiles, because Mom didn't need sadness—she needed love and peace and closure. I was so happy that I could give that to her and to her friends. I would love to have had a chance to say goodbye to my dad like that.

Not long after the Celebrate Sandra party, Mom started having pain in her right leg. We found out the cancer had gone into the femur, and she needed surgery to stabilize the bone.

The day after the bone cancer diagnosis, she said, "I guess this cancer's just going to eat me up."

Oh boy.

After the New Year, I felt like I needed to be home with my family. I hated leaving my mom, but I didn't know what to do. Naomi was taking on most of the responsibility for Lilo while Lance worked. It was too much.

The day before I left Mom, Dick came out to the house to talk about Mom's care. He couldn't help much because he worked, and he was a single dad. I was so frustrated I couldn't be in two places at once, and the frustration was easy to see.

"Come here, Honey," Mom said. "You've been here for me. I really appreciate everything you've done."

I flopped myself on the couch next to her. She put her arms around me and hugged me, and all I could think was how small she was. I felt like I might crush her. She was withering away. My mom . . . my mom was dying.

Mom decided to go to Arizona to live in her trailer and continue chemo. She lived in a beautiful over-fifty-five community, which was perfect for her. She would sit in her trailer and watch TV until she went to bed. I'd be there as much as I could. Sometimes I would leave my girls there to hang out with her while I ran errands.

I later found out that Naomi was adversely impacted by that decision. She was so afraid her grandma would die while she was there. She was seventeen years old. I thought she'd be fine, but I guess she wasn't.

Much of Lilo's care continued to fall on Naomi during this time. She was driving her all over the place and making meals and keeping things moving. My husband did what he could when he wasn't working, and I did what I could when I was home. Naomi also helped with my mom when she could. It was a stressful time, and I had little to give to my kids or my husband apart from basic daily needs.

Naomi was suffering, as she loved her grandmother. They were very close because my mom had spent a lot of time with her as a little girl when I was single and working. Naomi was affectionate and loving toward her grandparents. She loved spending time with them.

As we approached the end of my mom's life, I moved her into a small house for people who needed twenty-four-hour care. The hospice nurse suggested we move her there since she could no longer be left alone. Mom didn't want to move, but she wasn't safe alone. I visited her every day but one, and she made sure to let me know it.

The cancer had moved to her brain—we could tell by the way she was acting. She said outrageous things, stared out in space, and slept a lot.

The day before she died, she got to smoke her last cigarette; see Tula, her dog; and visit with me and the girls. I kissed her in her bed, checked on her oxygen, tucked Tula under my arm, and turned off the lights. And that was the last time I saw Mom alive.

The next morning, the hospice nurse called and said something had happened, and I should come. I didn't think she had died because the nurse would have said that. My brother called while I was driving over, so I was on the phone with him when I arrived. I was smiling because I didn't know. Everyone in the house looked sad. I only remember that in retrospect. The vibe was definitely unsettling. We went into Mom's room, and she was in her bed, but she was gone.

I told my brother Mom had died, and I leaned over and kissed her on the cheek and said, "Bye, Mom. I love you."

As I sat there in the silent room, waiting for the coroner to arrive, I was fascinated by my mom's body. It was her . . . it looked like her, but it wasn't her. She was no longer in the room with me. She had moved on to another place, and only her shell was left behind.

I drove back to Utah by myself to prepare my mom's funeral service and to clean out my childhood home to get it ready to sell. I had made that long drive from Utah to Arizona with an alive and breathing Mom just two months before. Now all that was left was a bag of ashes in the backseat of my car.

Both of my parents had been cremated. My dad was sprinkled on his golf course by his buddies, and the rest of him was buried in a beer can in the backyard. Mom's ashes were sprinkled on the beach of Antelope Island. She said she spent most of her life looking out at that island, and that was where she wanted to be left.

I slept in my parents' bedroom with the window open so I could hear the sound of the creek that babbled next to our house. It was a familiar sound, but since this was the last time I would be in this place, with this sound and this feeling, I tried to memorize it every night before I fell asleep.

Lance and the kids came up for the funeral. Naomi was singing the song her grandmother requested, "How Great Thou Art."

Before the funeral began, Naomi's biological grandpa came up to her, surprising us all.

Her aunt was with him. "We heard your grandma died," she said, "so we thought it would be a good chance to see you."

Detached, Naomi hugged them. They exchanged pleasantries, but as she walked away, she looked visibly shaken.

I pulled her aside. "What's going on? What's wrong?"

"How am I supposed to sing for Grandma now? They just show up out of nowhere and expect me to . . . what do they want? Why are they here?" She fought back tears. She was spiraling.

I put my hands on her shoulders and looked into her eyes. "Naomi, take a breath. They wanted to see you, and

I guess they thought this was a good way to do it. You can talk to them after the funeral. For now, if you still want to sing, try to focus on Grandma and the beautiful song you're going to sing for her. I know you can do this, but you don't have to if you're not up to it."

She stepped back and shook her head. "No, no. I want to do this for Grandma. I can do it."

"I know you can."

She did a lovely job. Grandma would have been proud of her.

The funeral was at the church my mom frequented. It was beautiful and well attended. Her canasta ladies were there as well as friends of mine and my brother's.

After the funeral most of the group went back to the house for food and drinks. We congregated in the living room and reminisced—about the time my mom stopped in the middle of a party to soothe an angry, crying teenager as she stomped through the house and threw herself on my parents' bed; the beer can collection; the football parties.

The Mormon friends chuckled at the memory of my dad always offering them a beer when they came to the house and all the funny things my dad said; how my mom was his perfect straight woman; and how she would get some good zingers in there sometimes. It was such a beautiful time of remembering not only my parents but my whole life. My parents were loved and engaged, and they were interesting people. I appreciated hearing how they touched all these lives. They will be remembered for many years through others' memories, and that makes my heart happy.

Funeral number three . . . check.

Part 2

Finding Me

Chapter 26

Storm Clouds Gathering

My relationship with Naomi was deteriorating. She had a really hard time with my mom dying. She didn't tell us she was having a hard time, but as I look back, I should have gotten her into some type of therapy to deal with her grief. When Mom would come stay at our house for the winter, Naomi would join her in the early morning, before school began, to watch *Matlock*. They were a lot alike. Same kind of temperament, easy to offend, prideful, people-pleasers.

Mom died when Naomi was seventeen years old and should have been getting ready to launch as an adult. Her dad and I had been talking to her about college, trade school, jobs. We tried and tried to get her to look at her future. Actually, we just tried to get her to get a job. She was complacent and evasive and downright disobedient. She resisted looking for a job, and when she did look, she wouldn't follow through.

She also started to resist her musical opportunities. She wouldn't practice before a performance, and she started to resent her part in whatever musical she was in. It seemed like everything she enjoyed in her life became a nuisance, and the harder she resisted it, the more I badgered, and the more we fought.

Every time I tried to talk to her, it ended up in a fight. I tried to reason with her, tried to make her remember "us"—her-and-me-against-the-world—but all I got back from her was anger and silence. She was not the child I thought I had raised. We had been inseparable, best friends, always talking. Now it seemed that every little thing was a problem and ended up in hurt feelings, tears, or slammed doors, often with no explanation. No matter how hard I tried to get her to talk to me, she wouldn't.

I understand it's normal for teens to behave this way as they are getting ready to leave the nest. Stay with me— there is more to this story.

One day, she informed her dad and me that she was go- ing to move out. She had been invited by the mother of one of her friends to live with them. I didn't know this woman very well, and what I knew I didn't like. I was sure Naomi was bad-mouthing her father and me and that was why this woman invited her to move in—to get away from the mon- strous parents. It was so embarrassing—and a lie! I was so angry, I got in my car, drove to the church parking lot, and cried and screamed until I couldn't breathe. I called Lory, a good listener, and told her what was going on.

She listened to me while I ranted. I was out of my mind. I was losing my best friend, the only person who loved me and accepted me. That one person who would be with me for all time. She was deserting me, leaving me alone in this world. I wanted to die. I had lost my one reason for living, and I was honestly praying for death to take me. I felt like this was the worst thing that had ever happened to me in my life. My worst fear had come to pass. I was alone, rejected by the one person I had grown and groomed to love me. I was nothing without her. I had no life without her. It was time for me to die.

Lory prayed with me.

I went home and talked with Naomi. She finally told me what was going on with her. Lance and I had been bugging her to get a job because she had graduated from school, and it was time. She didn't want to get a job because she thought she was going to be discovered at any moment, and she had to be home for that. She realized how irrational that sounded, and we were able to come to a peaceful way forward. She decided not to leave. I thought that was that.

But there was more to come.

Chapter 27

Patterns

Sometime after that night, I was invited to go to Atlanta, Georgia, to assist in the making of a documentary. I'd been going to college for filmmaking and was lucky to get the offer—a good opportunity.

I was in the airport waiting to board the plane, going over the events of the last little while in my mind. I was thinking about the mess with my daughter and about codependency and what it all meant. Lory was familiar with codependency. She had been involved in various recovery groups over the years, so I'd heard her talk about recovery and codependency for a long time. I remember hearing about a book called *Codependent No More,* so I went to the airport bookstore and found it.

I devoured the book on my trip, answering all the questions at the end of each chapter. I saw myself in the behaviors and the lives portrayed in the book. The picture started coming together with every chapter and every question I answered. I started to see how being codependent affected every relationship in my life, and I wanted to change. I was so happy there was an answer, and I was happy to do it.

My codependency was confirmed to me when I got home from Atlanta. I was playing *Dance, Dance Revolution* on the Wii with Naomi. She decided she didn't want to play anymore, so I asked Lilo to play with me.

She did a song or two, and when she wanted to stop playing, I said, in my best whiny voice, "Awww . . . Lilo, come on! You never want to do anything with me!"

"Mom! I am *not* going to be codependent with you like you are with Naomi!" she yelled as she stomped down the hall.

Whoa. Wake-up call! I realized at that moment that I didn't want to put these ugly behaviors on Lilo, and the only way I could make a difference was to break the cycle. That was when I started Celebrate Recovery.

Lory was deeply involved in Celebrate Recovery, a Christian recovery group with God as the only higher power. It was held at my church, so I was well aware of it, but Lory had never invited me to come. Celebrate Recovery is set up like an AA group, except the focus is on the Bible and Jesus. He is our higher power and our source for healing and recovery. I did homework every day and then met with my group every week to share our insights and report on where we were emotionally. No one was allowed to interact with the speaker by handing them a tissue or saying a consoling word. This practice is common for recovery groups, but it's extremely hard to do, especially for a codependent who wants to fix everyone.

I decided I was going to throw myself fully into this process and get better, once and for all. I went to all the meetings, did all my homework, and met with my sponsor. It was tough work, but I did it, and I am not exaggerating to say it was one of the best things I ever did for myself. I was in the recovery process during everything that happened that year and was glad I had the tools in the coming years, as I would need them. CR helped me process those difficult emotions in a healthy and supported way.

CR changed my life. It changed my marriage and my relationships. Since recovery is a multilayered process, I am still encountering situations in my life that reveal another wound in another layer. I welcome those times because I can work my recovery, find my wound, take it to God, work the steps, and free myself from another hurt.

Well, at least those are the things I do when I'm working my recovery. It's a lifetime discipline, and I forget, remember, and redo. A lot! I'm so thankful I went through this program when I did because it got me through the coming years.

Naomi would start relationships with one boy after another, trying to find someone to take care of her. One of the boys was in college, so she would sit on campus, waiting to hang with him between classes. If a boy worked, she'd be there before and after work, inserting herself in his life but not having or pursuing any life of her own.

She would go through phases of searching for a life for herself. One time she was going to go to college, once to a missionary school, another time to community college. She jerked us around until finally, Lance told her she had to either get a job, or he would put her to work at the house, eight hours of work, working for him. That lasted about a day before she got a job at Walmart giving out samples.

Actually, I got that job for her. I found every job for her. I wanted her to get working and get moving on with her life, and since I was so enmeshed, if she was unhappy, I had to fix it. I know—I hear it! More codependency, a reminder of all I had been through with Naomi's biofather—all that didn't work, that I didn't want but couldn't seem to quit.

Eventually, she got a job with Starbucks, and that was where she met Jack, the man who was going to take care of her. He was eighteen years older than she was, and she thought he was established, everything she wanted in a man—someone who would take on all the responsibility so she wouldn't have to, who would provide for her so she wouldn't have to do it herself. It was a relationship built on everything wrong—two people needing each other for all the wrong reasons and thinking they could change each other.

So of course, they went ahead and got engaged.

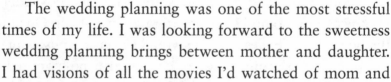

The wedding planning was one of the most stressful times of my life. I was looking forward to the sweetness wedding planning brings between mother and daughter. I had visions of all the movies I'd watched of mom and daughter picking out the wedding dress, sampling the cake, throwing the wedding shower, and sharing sweet memories.

None of that happened.

All I can say about this wedding was thank God for my friends. My friend Heather provided the dress, my friend

Corinne threw the shower, and my friend Lark and her family, including her husband, threw the reception.

Naomi was being so difficult and uncooperative. I didn't even think about the reception, except to order cupcakes, until Lark started asking me about it days before the wedding. It wasn't long before she realized if she didn't take over, it was going to be a disaster.

We had family and friends coming in from all over the country. Naomi wouldn't talk to me, wouldn't tell me her plans or what was going on with her, and if I needed information, it would be a fight. I was overwhelmed. Like I said, thank God for my friends.

Naomi was not happy about planning the wedding. She stomped around the house and was resistant to every part of it. She didn't want to buy the bridesmaid presents, and I nearly had to force her to get me a guest list or to address the invitations. And the dress—well, let me tell you about the dress.

Heather offered her wedding dress to Naomi. The dress was from her wedding thirty years ago, so it was vintage and exactly Naomi's size and taste. I brought it home for her to try on, and she refused to let me see it on her. I let it slide, but when Lark was over at the house, I told her about the dress and how I hadn't seen it on Naomi yet. Lark called Naomi to the kitchen and told her to get her dress on and to come out and show us.

Naomi made a fuss, and then Lark held out the dress. "Naomi! Go put your dress on and come out here. We need to check it to see if it needs altering. Go!"

Naomi grabbed the dress from Lark's hands and ran down the hall to her bedroom.

"Wow. Thanks," I said.

The dress fit her perfectly, and she looked lovely, but her attitude sucked!

I tried to talk to Naomi numerous times about calling off the wedding because I could tell she was not getting along with Jack, and I feared this marriage would be a disaster.

A day or two before the wedding, Naomi was clomping through the living room, and I said, "Naomi. You don't have to marry him. There's still time to call off the wedding."

She stopped. "Mom! I am going to marry this man . . ." It felt like she made herself stop before she said the rest of it: *I am going to marry this man . . . even if it kills me.*

I had people coming out from all over the country. I needed to get my house clean and ready for the after-party. Lance's whole family was coming out, and I didn't want my mother-in-law to see my house a mess. I put the need out there, and a team of five friends showed up at my door, some of them with buckets and cleaning supplies in tow. They descended on my house, scrubbing, cleaning, scouring, and even moving furniture. They had it done in no time, leaving me close to tears and grateful beyond words.

An hour before the wedding was supposed to start, Naomi decided she wanted to wear a particular necklace, so we were all scrounging through her storage unit looking for it, making us late for her hair and makeup. I can't remember if she found what she needed, but it was not the sweet, loving, memorable time I had hoped for. It was so hectic all I can remember is walking down the aisle, sitting in the front, and watching the vows.

My friend Chad was sitting across the way from me. He told me later he could see the relief come over me the minute they said their "I dos." He was right. I was relieved. She was not my problem anymore.

The reception was lovely, thanks to Lark and her crew. And then the best part—the after-party, Everyone came to my house, and we had the best time! We ate the left-over cupcakes, drank sangria, and danced. My nephews were swing dancing with all the ladies, from ages seven to seventy-seven. I could finally relax for the first time in *so* many months.

It was the sweetest gift for me to sit and enjoy my family and friends, people I hadn't seen in years, friendships developed since childhood, and the new friends who had come to my rescue in my time of need. I was so blessed to have that time—that after-party—to remind me of the beauty of life, the relationships that worked, the love passed between people who just loved you because you were you and not because of what you could do for them. It was one of the best times of my life, and I will never forget it.

Chapter 28

No Relief

After she was married, Naomi wanted us to do Christmas together with her in-laws, and it wasn't fun. We'd have to go to Naomi and Jack's house, and his parents and sister and her girlfriend would be there watching television.

The first year I had to ask them to please mute the TV so we could open presents. They wouldn't play games with us, and it was just awkward, but we went because we were trying to keep the peace and keep the doors open.

Most of the time when we saw Naomi and Jack, it was contentious. Jack acted like he was better than us, and he wouldn't join in with our family. Whenever they came over for dinner, Jack would eat and then go into the living room, refusing to play cards with us. I always invited him to play, but he didn't want to, so I didn't push it. We honestly tried to include him in our family, but he was determined not to be included.

I knew the marriage was not going well. Naomi wouldn't tell me much, but there were indications she could not hide, like any day she was with me or her sister and she wasn't at home at the exact moment he told her to be home, he would text her incessantly. I heard him talk to her, loud and stern, over the phone, and on one very rare occasion when the girls and I went to Utah for a quick trip, when we got home, Naomi texted me:

> You wouldn't believe the
> crazy I came home to.

The frustrating thing for me was that she wouldn't talk to me about what was going on. She'd get mad if I asked the wrong question or challenged her on something she said about herself or her marriage. It was excruciating to have a conversation with her. It was fake and surface and so, so sad.

One day after a year of awkward silences, forced conversations, and angry comments, I asked, "Naomi, what happened to us? We were so close your whole life up until, well, I guess since your grandmother died. What happened to 'you and me against the world'?"

I don't remember exactly what she said, but it was clear she didn't want anything to do with our "close" relationship. I guess it was so hurtful to me that I blocked it out. It was just so confusing, though, because she would be welcoming to me one moment and rejecting the next. It was this push-pull thing she would do with me, and it made me crazy!

About eighteen months after Naomi's wedding, I

was driving home from a Christian women's retreat, and Naomi called me in hysterics. Jack took the phone from her. "Could you please come over here? Naomi needs you."

I was so surprised she would come to me because of the way she'd been treating me, but I hurried over there as soon as I could.

As I walked in the front door, she screamed, "I'm pregnant!"

She began mumbling things about how she didn't want this to happen, and she didn't want a baby, and how could this happen to her. I just stood there and listened. Naomi and Jack had said they didn't want children, but I knew it wasn't true for Naomi. She had always wanted kids! She was good with them and loved them. I knew she was just lying to herself, so I don't know if her reaction was for Jack's benefit or if she was just scared.

I hugged her and told her everything was going to be all right. I didn't know what else to say. It was a done deal.

As I drove away from the house, I thought, again, how it felt like Naomi had ruined everything good and fun about having an adult child. The wedding had been stressful, and we all just couldn't wait for it to be over with, and now she was pregnant. I was going to be a grandmother, and she had ruined that for me too.

No sweet baby reveal, no surprise, or "Mom, you're going to be a grandmother!" Everything I had ever wanted or dreamed of for my adult child, all the sweet experiences, were taken away from me. She made sure of it, whether it was intentional or not.

It felt intentional.

Naomi didn't let me be involved with the pregnancy at

all—surprise, surprise. She let me go to one prenatal visit and one baby shower. She was cold and distant when she came around, and it was getting worse.

One day when Naomi was about six months pregnant, she and Jack came over to the house. Jack went into the garage to borrow some tools from Lance, and Naomi sat on the couch.

"Mom, I have something to talk to you about. In my childbirth class, the teacher said that if I was holding anything against anyone, it would be good for me to work it out before I go into labor."

I sat down next to her and turned my body toward hers. "Okay. Sounds like a good idea."

"I didn't think I had anything, but then later, Jack and I were taking a walk, and he asked if I had any problems with you, if I was holding anything against you. I realized I *was* mad at you, for making me sit with Grandma when she was sick."

I sat quietly listening.

She continued. "I was so nervous sitting with her when you were gone. I was afraid she was going to die while I was with her, and I would go check on her while she was sleeping every five minutes. I was so worried every time you left me with her. I don't think you should have made me do that!"

"Okay, I'm sorry, Honey." Then, feeling a bit defensive, I continued, "You were seventeen years old, and Dad and I thought you were old enough to help the family through this difficult time. I understand. It was a choice your dad and I made, and maybe you'll make a different choice with your children, but we don't believe in keeping our children from the tough things of life. Death is part of life, and this was your chance to experience it with some-one you loved. You never said anything to me, so I didn't know you were having a hard time with it. As far as I knew, you were happy to spend time with her."

"I just wish she hadn't died." She cried.

"I know. Me too! But I couldn't stop it. No one could." I closed the space between us and hugged her. "Will you forgive me?"

I could barely hear her words as she muttered them in my shoulder. "Yeah, I forgive you."

Chapter 29

Tension Builds

Naomi continued to withhold herself as much as she could from me concerning her marriage and the baby. I felt like it was her way of punishing me for something she was still holding against me. She did tell us she was having a girl and her due date, but when she went into labor, she told her husband not to tell us. He texted us anyway, at about 3:00 a.m., and told us she was laboring at home in the tub as planned.

The next morning, I had a date with Corinne for breakfast, so I kept the date and was at the table eating when Jack called again to tell me Naomi had had the baby, and all was well. They asked if I'd bring them a hamburger from In-N-Out.

Corinne and I picked up the burgers and made our way over to the house. We walked into the bedroom, and

Jack handed me a blanket with this tiny baby in it. I was elated! I was a grandmother! Wow . . . I was a grandmother. So hard to believe.

I took the baby in my arms and laid her on the bed. I opened up the blanket to see her little body, and as I scanned down, I saw something quite unexpected! A penis! It was a boy! They had been wrong all along, and we had a boy! I squealed!

"Oh my heck! What am I going to do with you?"

I'd never had boys and was frankly scared of them. Then he started to cry while everyone else was laughing. I picked him up and held him to my chest and explained to him how we were going to figure it out together, and that I loved him more than I could ever imagine. His name was Kirk, and he was perfect!

A month later, Jack confessed to being an alcoholic and admitted he needed to go into rehab. He went into a thirty-day program and left Naomi home alone with a tiny baby. She seemed to be doing fine on her own, because even though I offered my help, she never wanted it.

During this time, Lance, Lilo, and I were heading off to Missouri for a Rohlf family reunion. It was an inopportune time for us to leave because Jack was in rehab, Naomi was alone, and our family dog, Goliath, was having heart trouble. We took him to the vet, and he put him on medicine, but Goliath wasn't doing so great. It was a quandary, but we finally decided to go. Naomi seemed fine on her own, and we left Goliath with a dog sitter.

We were at the Hard Rock Café in St. Louis having dinner, just the three of us. We had finished giving our order to a surly waitress when I got a phone call from Lara, our dog sitter.

"Hi, Lara. Is everything okay?"

"Michelle, I couldn't find Goliath when I got to the house. He didn't greet me like he usually does, and then I found him in the back corner of the yard. He's not breathing well."

"Oh, poor baby. Please take him to the animal hospital and call Naomi so she can pay for the visit."

"Okay, thanks." The line went dead.

Not long after the first call, we got a call from the veterinarian. Lance and I moved outside on the porch to take the call. Our food had not arrived yet.

"Goliath's heart is failing. We can put him on drugs, but he's not going to last much longer either way. I might be able to keep him alive until you get home, but he's struggling. What would you like me to do?"

Lance and I had already discussed what we would do if it came to this point, so we told the vet to let Goliath go. We called Naomi and asked her to be with our sweet dog—her pet—a big deal, for sure, while he died, and then went back to our table to break the news to Lilo. The grumpy waitress approached with our food to a tableful of crying customers.

"Could you please pack up the food? We just found out our dog died."

She immediately softened.

We called Naomi later and asked how it had gone.

"I walked into the vet and said goodbye to Goliath. The vet asked if I wanted to stay while he gave Goliath the drugs, and I said I didn't, so I paid the bill and left."

No emotion, no tears, rote commentary. I wondered how it must have felt to walk into the vet's office with a month-old baby in her arms, husband and family gone, and have to put the dog down, alone. She never said a word, so I guessed it wasn't a big deal for her, but looking back on it now, I think it was.

Jack was out of rehab for about a month before he stopped going to AA meetings and started acting like he was drinking again. His counselor recommended Naomi tell Jack she was seeing old behaviors and he needed to get back into AA and attend his appointments with his counselor, or she would have to leave him. He didn't do it, so Naomi asked if she could move back in with us until he got his act together.

They stayed with us for six weeks or a month. I'm not sure how long, but it was torture. Naomi would vacillate between being my friend and treating me like I was her worst enemy. She wouldn't talk to Jack, so Jack had to communicate child arrangements through Lance. Jack was unhappy and angry, so he didn't speak to Lance in a respectful tone, and then Naomi was upset and frustrated and couldn't decide what to do.

Another part of the dynamic of her coming back into the house was the way Naomi would enlist Lilo in undermining me. Naomi would whisper about me to Lilo, who, with teenage angst in full swing, would naturally side with her sister. They wouldn't necessarily do it in front of me, but I could tell they were making fun of me or texting about me, sometimes right in front of my face.

One day while I was driving Lilo to her job, we got into a fight about something she and Naomi had said about me. As it escalated, I got more and more upset. Once she got out of the car, I called Lance, hysterical.

"I need you to be ready to talk to me when I get home!" I yelled-sobbed. "The girls were talking about me, and I am so sick of them ganging up on me!"

You might be wondering why I would care that my children were talking about me. Well, if I had been emotionally healthy, I probably wouldn't have, but I had my own gaping wounds of rejection and abandonment. The people who were supposed to love me were being the perpetrators of a lifelong experience of the "mean girl" phenomenon, and they were in my own home! It was too much for me to bear.

I couldn't wait until she moved out. I couldn't wait to have my peaceful home back. I couldn't wait for my life to return to normal.

She moved out, but things didn't return to normal—not for a very long time. Well . . . ever.

Once Naomi returned to her home, Jack decided he would go back to school and get his master's degree in addiction counseling. While Jack was in school, Naomi went to work to support them. They asked me if I would watch Kirk three days a week. I agreed, happy to spend time with him. It was fun having Kirk around, watching him develop through the first year. I saw his first steps and heard some of his first words. He was a sweet boy, and we loved him.

Naomi and Jack were very unhappy—mostly Naomi—so the pickups and drop-offs were not fun. They were grouchy and argumentative most of the time. I tried to get Naomi to talk to me, but she wouldn't share anything real about her life. She'd talk about work or other people, but never what was going on with her and Jack. It was even worse than before. It seemed like after she went back to him, he made her promise to never talk to us about her life with him. They quit spending time with us at all, except for holidays, and even then, there was tension in the air whenever they were around.

One afternoon, Jack came to pick Kirk up. He was clearly in an argumentative mood. He started out complaining about his wife, my daughter, saying how she wasn't doing enough, how she was not keeping the house clean or cooking enough. He complained about her being depressed and sitting on the couch.

I gently defended her, not wanting to upset him and make his mood worse. When he realized I wasn't going to agree with him, he turned on me. He started criticizing the way I was taking care of Kirk.

I countered with positive remarks, just trying to get the conversation finished so he would go home. It was one of those conversations I knew I wasn't going to win. He was trying to pick a fight, and it wasn't working.

He finally left after stomping around and changing Kirk's diaper and accusing me of not changing it often enough, even though I was the one who had fixed Kirk's diaper rash many times. I wish I had stopped talking from the beginning, because it was clear he was out to punish me, and trying to explain myself or rationalize with him didn't help.

The punishment would be severe.

Chapter 30

Do You See What I See?

The next week, Naomi and Jack were at the house picking Kirk up. We had been watching him for about nine months, three days a week, with very little input from his parents.

A short time after this last encounter, Naomi said, "Mom, you don't have to watch Kirk anymore. I am going to change my work schedule so I can watch him."

"Oh! Okay. Starting when?" I asked.

She seemed nervous to tell me, which was perplexing to me. I was happy for her. I knew she wanted to be home with her son.

"Right away. I can start right away."

"Okay! Sounds good to me!"

In retrospect, this was a deliberate move toward our eventual estrangement. From that day on, we saw Kirk very little.

Naomi was already ignoring me the best she could, celebrating her dad's birthday with dinner and cards at her house and then totally forgetting my birthday. Father's Day was recognized with presents and a stop to the house; Mother's Day was ignored except for a snail-mailed card from Kirk, which I loved!

Every time she ignored me or dismissed me, I screamed inside, "What is wrong with you?" She was my life, and she was outright rejecting me, not caring about my feelings at all! It happened so consistently, I stopped expecting anything different from her. Every time she came to the house, she would hug Lilo, then Lance, and then she'd turn away.

One time, Naomi and a friend came by the house to attend a Bible study I was teaching. There were about ten women in my living room when they arrived. She was sure to talk to and hug every woman in the room, all the while not looking at me and barely acknowledging I was in the room, even though I was talking to and interacting with her and her friend. Her rejection of me was so obvious a couple of women came up to me after Naomi left to ask me if everything was okay.

Lory, whom I had shared a lot of this situation with, said, "Michelle! How can you let her get away with that? She is awful to you!"

"What am I supposed to do? She's an adult. She can do what she wants. She does this all the time. She'll come to the house and hug her dad and sister and walk away. She has been punishing me ever since her grandma died. I've tried to talk to her, and she says nothing is wrong and that I'm crazy and reading things into it. I'm just so glad you noticed. Now I know I'm not crazy, at least about this!"

The estrangement year, as I call it, started slowly but accelerated as the year went on. Things I had been able to do with Kirk in the past were no longer allowed. For instance, taking him for a playdate with a fellow grandma and her grandson, being invited for Halloween, or taking him to see the Christmas lights. Lance and I were seeing the baby less and less, except for the occasional times Jack or Naomi would invite us to meet them at the park. Naomi would do gymnastics to make sure I didn't see Kirk.

One day she and Jack had an overlap in schedules, so instead of asking me to watch him for the time in between, she took him to work in his pajamas and called her sister to come get him from her at her work to take him to Jack. I had asked Lilo to stop by the house to pick up a pan for Naomi. I handed her the pan and talked to Kirk for a while. As soon as Lilo was two minutes late, Jack started texting her. Lilo explained they were at my house and that I was talking to Kirk. Jack started badgering Lilo, demanding she get Kirk home immediately.

I had been suggesting to my husband for some time that they were intentionally keeping us away from the baby or not allowing us to be alone with him, but he didn't want to believe it. He wanted to give them the benefit of the doubt, saying they were just trying to make their way.

After so many circumstances like this, he was finally seeing what I was seeing.

Chapter 31

Grudges and Gravy

We were hosting Thanksgiving at our house. Naomi and her family planned to come over for dinner. They showed up two hours before they had said they would and pretty much took over the kitchen.

Naomi and Lilo were talking and laughing and whispering to each other while they cooked, taking over the preparations Lance and I had started. I wasn't really upset about it because I don't like to cook anyway, so when Naomi said she would do the potatoes and the casserole, I was fine with it.

The atmosphere was definitely strained, but I didn't dwell on it because I was playing with my grandson. Once we sat down to eat, the table was intermittently filled with silence and small talk. At the beginning of the meal, Naomi asked if we had gluten-free gravy. We didn't. I had forgotten she had mentioned needing gluten-free gravy in an earlier conversation. I could feel the tension, and I knew there was something going on, but I couldn't imagine what it could be. So I just focused my attention on the baby and enjoyed the meal and the family the best I could.

A week later, I was driving to Tucson, Arizona, with Lory for a weekend away when I got a phone call from Naomi.

"Hi!" I said. "I'm driving to Tucson. How are you?"

"Mom, Thanksgiving wasn't fun for us."

"I'm sorry." I looked at Lory, confused.

"I told you I needed gluten-free gravy, and you didn't provide any for me, so I couldn't have gravy on my potatoes, and then you weren't ready to eat when we showed up. We had to do all the cooking because you weren't done!"

"Naomi, I am sorry I forgot the gluten-free gravy. This gluten issue is brand new to me," I said. "You never told me you had a gluten issue until you mentioned to me you needed gluten-free gravy days before dinner. I'm sorry I forgot." My defense ramped. "And as far as us not being ready for you, *you were two hours early!* No! We were *not* ready for you! We had our own plans, and you showed up, interrupting *our* plans for the day. We graciously *allowed* you to take over our kitchen!"

No matter what I said, she insisted we had been inconsiderate and irresponsible and had ruined her Thanksgiving. After her accusations and my apology, there was nothing left to say. I knew something was really wrong with my daughter and her husband. The only thing I could track back to was that day when Jack came home super grouchy and blamed me for not changing Kirk's diaper. That was really the last interaction we had before they terminated our babysitting privileges and stopped coming around. I tried to talk to Naomi about it many times, and she would just say I was crazy, or they were busy. I never got anywhere with her, and when I tried Jack, it was all accusations and excuses. They reeked of anger and resentment when they were around us.

It was worse every time we saw them, but they wouldn't talk about it or try to work it out with us. They harbored every perceived slight, every resentment, every judgment and stowed them in their "bags" to pull out and make their case to each other of what awful, dangerous, dysfunctional people we were.

The more they talked about it, nurturing their litany of offenses, the stronger the hold the offenses had on them, and the more it permeated the air between us. The toxic pressure was building, and it was about to blow.

Chapter 32

Ugly Christmas

Sometime in early December, Naomi called and asked us to watch Kirk for an hour so she and Jack could go to his work Christmas party. We were thrilled she had called, despite knowing that we were probably their last resort. We were thankful to spend time with him.

They showed up at our doorstep all dressed up and ready for a party. Kirk came into the house and made himself at home, finding the toys he had at our house.

I asked about food, and Naomi said, "He just had a cookie, so he probably won't eat, but you can try if you'd like."

"Okay," I said. "Dad was about to get out some blueberries, and he usually loves eating blueberries with Papa. I'm also making cookies, so he can help me."

"We won't be gone long. No longer than an hour," Jack said. "We better go."

Kirk and I finished making the no-bake cookies I had started, and then we put him in the truck and took him around the neighborhood to look at Christmas lights while the cookies cooled. When we got home, we walked around the neighborhood, looking at the lights and talking.

"What's this, Mimi?" He pointed a chubby finger at a broken reindeer in a neighbor's yard display.

"I think that's a moose. Kinda looks like a moose to me, but—"

"It's a reindeer." Lance interrupted. "I think it's broken, and that's why it looks strange."

"Reindeer!" Kirk proclaimed. "Broken reindeer. Right, Papa?"

"Yeah, I think so."

We had just walked in the door when Naomi and Jack got there. Naomi saw the cookies on the counter, and I guess she assumed I had given him a cookie, but I hadn't. They'd needed time to cool, and we had been gone the rest of the time.

Naomi and Jack seemed irritated when we told them we had taken Kirk out to see the Christmas lights and that we hadn't stayed in the house with him the entire time. They had never given us any instruction not to take him out, so I was surprised by the attitude. Nothing new, I guess. Still, I was just happy Lance and I had gotten to spend time with our grandson.

Shortly after the party, Naomi called.

Here we go again.

"Hi, Mom."

"Hi! How are you?"

"We're fine. We need to talk about Christmas," she said.

"Okay. I assume Jack's parents are coming into town, so what are we doing this year?"

"Well, we . . . Jack and his mom . . ." She was hedging. "Well, Jack's mom wants to have Christmas all to herself this year. She wants to decorate our house and make it all about her family and my family"—she was rambling—"so you can't see us on Christmas. We aren't going to see you on Christmas."

There it is.

"What about Christmas Eve?" I was hoping. "Could you come over and open presents on Christmas Eve, do you think?" I actually really expected the answer to be yes.

"No, Mom. Not Christmas Eve either," she blurted. "I thought we could open our Christmas presents over my birthday dinner at the restaurant."

"Okay. I guess." My stomach hurt. This was so unfair. "So, to be clear, you do not want to see us at all during Christmas, right?"

"Yes, that's right."

"Okay, see you at dinner. Bye." I tried not to let her hear my disappointment.

I wasn't broken up about not spending Christmas with Jack's family. We had been invited to do so for a couple of years, and it hadn't been fun for us. They didn't play games or talk or, really, do much of anything. We would float into the house, keep it surface and quick just to open presents, and then we'd float back out of the house and do our own Christmas Day fun, but without them.

The thing that upset me the most was that we had to do our Christmas present opening at a restaurant over a table. That was sad to me. It felt cold and formal. I really wanted to have Kirk open presents while his papa and I watched him and played with him. I was disappointed Naomi was taking that away from us.

Jack's family always took precedence. I never really minded it—I understood. We were in town, and they were not. But when the estrangement started and Jack's family became the preferred-family-at-all-times, I started feeling angry and resentful toward them, especially Jack's mom. I was perfectly happy to give most of the Christmas holiday to her because they were from out of town, but now she wanted every single second! That was just selfish and inconsiderate. So weird.

I was not okay with losing all of the Christmas holiday and only getting to open presents over a table in a restaurant. I cried for days before the dinner. I couldn't understand how this could happen. I was so accommodating to everyone in that family, and all they could do was want more, demand more, be offended more. I felt so angry and frustrated and lost. I had no reference for this brand of dysfunction in a family, and I didn't know how to handle it except the way I was handling it, and that was by trying to communicate and explore the feelings and opinions of the other person, and it wasn't working! I felt hopeless. I had a feeling of dread going into Naomi's birthday dinner. Things were escalating, and I could tell. I had no idea what was next, but I knew it wasn't going to be good.

And it wasn't.

After the call from Naomi about Christmas, I had the opportunity to pick Kirk up at Naomi's work and drop him off at the house with Jack. I can't remember why, except they must've been desperate. Anyway, I drove up to the house, and Jack met us outside. I jumped out of the car, took Kirk out of his car seat, hugged and kissed him, and put him down. Jack thanked me for bringing him home.

"You're welcome. Glad to do it. I guess we won't be seeing you until after the New Year, so have a good Christmas."

Jack looked confused and said, "Um . . . we . . . well, we could maybe bring Kirk down Christmas morning for a couple of minutes to open presents, if you'd like."

It dawned on me that he didn't know we weren't going to see them for Christmas. It was Naomi who didn't want us around, not Jack's mom or Jack. Oh. My. Heck!

"Naomi told me your mom wanted it to be just your family this year and that she wouldn't see us at all until next year."

"Oh. I, um . . . I think we could make it work to come by in the morning," he said.

"No, it's okay. When Naomi told us your plans for Christmas week, we made plans to go to Flagstaff. Thanks anyway."

I drove away knowing it wasn't okay—it was disappointing that we couldn't have a normal family.

One of the few traditions we had as a family was to go out to dinner for the person's birthday. They chose where they'd like to go, and we'd celebrate at that restaurant. Naomi's birthday dinner was a disaster for me. Naomi and Lilo sat on one side of the table whispering to each other. I hung out with Kirk on the other side, soaking up every minute I could with him. Lance and Jack made small talk at the other end of the table. We exchanged and opened our Christmas presents.

Lance got presents he would use and appreciate, like ammo and stuff for the travel trailer. Mine were impersonal and clearly regifted. I am not a "things" person, more a "thoughts" person, and I didn't feel like any thought was put into my presents at all! I even felt like they were spiteful, but that could have been where I was at that point. It had been a very long year.

At the end of the meal, Naomi ordered a key lime pie for her birthday. She took a bite and then passed it around to the rest of us to sample. I was the last one to take a bite, but when I was finished, I handed it back to her. She looked at me like I was insulting her and shook her head.

Perplexed, I asked, "You don't want any more pie?"

She shook her head at me. I didn't get it, but I put the pie down and shrugged it off.

Two days before Christmas, Naomi called and said she wanted to come over to get Kirk's last present from us. Since we weren't going to see Kirk for Christmas, I asked to have him come to the house to open his bigger present from us so we could play with him. Naomi said they had to do it at 5:00 p.m. sharp!

I called my husband and explained it was the only chance we had to see Kirk before Christmas. Thankfully, he was able to leave work early to join us.

The evening started out normal enough. Jack mumbled some kind of greeting and sprawled out on the couch. Naomi sat in a chair watching us play with Kirk. It wasn't long before Kirk got bored and moved to standing on the kitchen chair, playing with the light switches. That was something we let him do at our house. The adults were in the living room.

"We would love to have Kirk spend the night with us sometime, like he used to."

Jack sat up. "No, we don't think it's a good idea for Kirk to be around you without supervision."

"Why?" I wasn't shocked by his statement because I had the feeling that was what had been happening with them, only letting us see him at the park when one of them was with us. I was happy we were finally getting things out in the open. Maybe we could fix this thing.

"Well, because. When you were watching him, you didn't change his diaper that time, and you didn't put him to bed and wake him up on schedule like we asked."

At this point, Lance was standing in the kitchen, supervising Kirk as he climbed up and down the chair. He was engaged in the conversation, but not speaking. Naomi was standing too.

"Jack, I stayed on top of the diaper changing. Besides! Who was the one who repeatedly cured his diaper rash? It was me!" I wasn't emotional because I was sure we could work this out by listening to each other and being reasonable. I hoped we could clear the air and get all this tension out from between us.

I continued with the facts. "And as far as the sleep schedule, we tried to keep to it as closely as possible. I believe in schedules, and we did the best we could. But sometimes, kids don't do things exactly as you'd like them to. Sometimes Kirk had a hard time getting to sleep, sometimes he fell asleep early, sometimes he woke up early. If I let him sleep in, it was only for a half hour or so."

"Well, Lilo said you let him sleep in, and other times she would hear him crying because you hadn't picked him up from his bed yet," he accused.

"Yeah, that probably happened, Jack. I think I remember having to pee before I went to get him, and he was fussing. Lilo swooped in, picked him up, and accused me of not staying on schedule. Things can't go perfectly every time. They just don't. I'm sure you don't have every day go perfectly either." I was starting to get frustrated.

"You gave Kirk a cookie and then lied to us about it," he blurted.

"What! When?" I asked, looking at my husband for an answer.

Naomi said, "When we had you babysit for Jack's work Christmas party."

"Oh, no, I didn't give him a cookie that day. We made cookies, but we couldn't eat them because they had to sit for a while. By the time we got back from our walk, you arrived to pick him up. He never had a chance for a cookie." I explained. "Now that I think about it, you are the one who told me he wouldn't be hungry because he just ate a cookie."

"You haven't told the truth about any of it," Jack said.

"Are you calling us liars?" Lance's voice reverberated through the room.

Silence. All our eyes were on Jack, waiting for an answer to Lance's question.

"Yes, I am," he said.

"*Mom.*" It was Naomi. "I thought you would like it this way. You don't have to worry about changing his diaper or figuring out what food to feed him. You can just play with him and love him, and I'll do all the care."

"Because you don't think we can do it? We watched him three days a week for over a year, and you had no complaints, and all of a sudden you won't let us be with him without supervision? That's ridiculous!" I was starting to raise my voice.

This cannot be happening!

"You can spend time with him—just with me too," she explained.

"I don't want to spend time with you!" I spit. I'd lost my composure. "I don't understand why we can't spend time with him like we did before."

"Because you have problems with food. I told you not to give him a cookie, and you did and lied about it. Then you tried to make me eat the rest of my birthday pie."

"It was *your* pie!" Lance boomed.

I turned to Jack, snarling. "So sorry I can't be as perfect as your perfect mother. I'm sure your perfect mother will get to spend time alone with him!"

At that point the room went out of focus for me. Naomi was saying something; her voice sounded far away. My brain barely registering the words, I heard her say, "Let's go!"

I didn't see Jack pull Kirk off the chair or see how they got to the door. All I saw was Jack following Naomi out the front door with Kirk yelling for me over his dad's shoulder. I was so surprised they were running away that I stood at the door and pleaded to let him say goodbye to us, but they didn't let him. They didn't look back. They just got in the car and left.

I closed the door and quietly moved back into the room. My husband was standing beside me, looking shocked and, well . . . shocked. His family of origin was very calm and unassuming, so having all this drama and yelling and storming out was not in his toolbox. It wasn't in mine either. This behavior was an anomaly to us, and we were obviously at a loss as to how to handle it.

"What just happened? How did they . . . ? Why would they think we were so awful? Did you hear Naomi say I force-fed her her own pie? Jack accused me of lying! When have I ever lied to my kids? Why would I lie about a stupid cookie? I don't understand what went wrong! Why did it get so crazy? I can't believe that just happened!" I fast-pitched each question at my husband as each one occurred to me.

"I'm so sorry, honey. I was going to step in when he started accusing us of things, but then it sounded like you might work it out with him, so I stayed out of it until he called us liars."

"Oh. Yeah. It did seem like he might listen for a second, but then . . . it went bad, fast!" I sat down on the couch, shaking my head. *What is wrong with her?* "I can't believe Naomi would stand there and let him talk to us like that! Or that she would believe the things she was saying about us. I just can't believe it." Head still shaking.

Silence fell over our house as the two of us went over the evening's events. I knew we'd work it out sometime. Families work things out, and life goes on. We would be okay. I looked up to say something to my husband, and that was when I saw it. My husband—my big, burly, manly husband—was crying. I wasn't crying, and I was always the one who cried.

"Honey, what's wrong?"

"There's no coming back from this," he said, ignoring the tears falling down his cheeks into his beard. "I just don't see a way out of it. There's no coming back from this. None."

He cried on and off that whole evening. I know my own pain, but I can only imagine how he felt to have his daughter call him a liar in the home he had provided for her, to have his first grandson ripped away from him with words of anger and disdain. I can only imagine, because he never talked about it.

"There's no coming back from this."

His words echoed in my mind. He was absolutely, tragically correct.

Chapter 33

Radio Silence

We didn't hear anything from them the rest of December or January. Our topic of conversation was mostly about them and what had happened and what was to come. How would they contact us? Would they give us conditions? What kind of boundaries would they put up? Would we ask for anything or just be happy to go back to seeing the grandbaby? So many discussions, so many what-ifs. It was exhausting.

Then, toward the end of January, Lance and I saw a post from Jack and Naomi on Facebook announcing her pregnancy. It was yet another disappointment in a string of things Naomi made sure to ruin for me. Another baby, another stupid way of finding out. No sweet proclamations or fun reveals again. Just a post on Facebook.

She once again made it clear we were not special, and we were not part of her inner circle. She didn't value our relationship enough to tell us we were going to be grandparents again in person, let alone in a fun, celebratory way. We found out like all the other "friends" on her page.

There wasn't any joy for us. It was another slight—another way of Naomi letting us know that we were not important, and we didn't deserve any special treatment.

The next day I went to pull up the announcement again on Facebook to show someone else, and I couldn't find her page or Jack's. Lance and I had been unfriended. We no longer had access to either one of their pages. What children they were, I thought. They were really throwing a tantrum.

I was not hopeless at this point. I kept thinking Naomi would be coming back. She had always come back in the past. She would stay away for hours, maybe days, but then she'd pop up, pretending nothing had ever happened. No apologies or admission of wrongdoing, of course, but she'd come back smiling and talking as if everything were normal, with no thought to whether she had hurt someone's feelings or that her actions had affected someone.

As the months ticked by with no contact, I started feeling like we might be in for the long haul. I couldn't believe she would want to go through her pregnancy without our support. I couldn't believe she was living her life without us when she had been so close to us.

She had been one of those children who wanted to go everywhere with me. She wanted to be in the living room with the adults. She didn't like to be in her room like most teenagers and was very seldom alone. It was so hard to believe she was willing to throw her family away.

I was still thinking she was throwing a tantrum and would be back when things got tough, so I wasn't feeling the pain yet. But it was coming for me for sure.

One of the ways I dealt with the emptiness of my heart and my house was to turn to my two biggest idols, sugar and TV. I am not going to deny I have an issue with sugar. It has been my friend and comforter for most of my life. It's the thing I turn to when I am sad, lonely, confused, and insecure, as well as when I'm happy, joyful, and want to celebrate.

The difference between those two scenarios—the sad-and-lonely sugar eating versus the joyous-and-happy sugar eating—is the motivation behind it. When I am down in the dumps, I use sugar and TV to soothe me, to distract me from my emotions and my circumstances. It's a type of dis-association—a way of escape—and I understand it is not healthy. I acknowledge that fact, but I would never force someone else to eat with me. In fact, for the addiction to be fulfilling, it had to be done in isolation. Force-feeding children—or anyone—was never a part of the dysfunction.

It looked more like this: I would go to See's Candies, buy a half pound of chocolate, go home, sit in my rocking chair, and watch TV. It was my way of disassociating from the situation I found myself in. It just added to my misery, because every night before bed, I would stand in the bathroom and hate myself for treating my body that way. I'd feel sick and tired and sad, but it didn't stop me from getting those chocolates every day or two.

The loneliness was excruciating, and the chocolate and TV made it bearable.

Until it didn't.

Chapter 34

Precious Moments

In March, my church held a fundraiser in the parking lot. I signed up for a shift as cashier. On my way, I had a feeling I was going to see Naomi. The thought of seeing her and Kirk made me happy. I wasn't nervous or upset; I was excited to see them.

Sure enough, there they were, playing on the church playground—Naomi, Kirk, and Lilo. I jumped out of the car, not wanting anyone to move before I could get my hands on that little boy. I ran onto the playground, so excited, and hugged and kissed both my girls, and then Kirk came running toward me.

"Mimi!"

"Hi, sweetheart! How are you? What are you doing?" I hugged him tight. It was so good to see him!

"Come play!" He grabbed my hand and led me toward the slide.

I looked back at Naomi and noticed she was nervous. She was walking back and forth, talking, and gesturing wildly with her hands to her sister. I wondered for a moment what might be going on there, but since I didn't know if I was ever going to see my grandson again, I put my focus back on him.

"You ready? Come on down!" Kirk landed in my arms. I stood up and looked into his eyes. "I love you. Always remember, Kirk, Mimi and Papa love you, and we always will." I kissed him on the cheek and put him down.

"Mom." Naomi was standing next to me.

"Hi!" I said, looking around for Kirk, who had found his way to his Aunt Lilo.

"Could we go to get a meal or something? Me and Jack, and you and Dad? Can we try and talk this all out? I mean, can we sit down and have a meal?"

"Sure, Naomi."

She was hyped up, which made me speak calmly and evenly. "Your dad and I would be happy to talk with you two. We always have been. You were the ones who ran out that night. We figured when you were ready to communicate with us, you would."

"Could we just get together for a meal or something? I think it's our men. If we could get the men together and talk. . . I don't think it's us. I think we want to be okay, don't we? I mean, could we just have a meal together?"

She was still talking fast, and I felt she was trying to reach out the best way she knew.

"Of course, Naomi. I think Dad would be more comfortable with coffee than with a meal."

"Okay. How about tomorrow?"

"Sure. You text us the time and the place, and we'll be there." I saw Kirk running toward me.

"Okay, good." Then to Kirk she said, "Kirk, we gotta get going pretty soon."

Kirk grabbed my hand and led me back to the slide. "Mimi! Slide!"

I cherished every single moment with him during that brief time, and I'm so glad I did.

Chapter 35

"Intervention"

Lance and I talked about the meeting all evening. I was hopeful, remembering Naomi's stated intention of working things out between all of us. He and I discussed what our issues were and realized we really didn't have any except that they had accused us of lying and then stopped talking to us.

We decided not to even bring up the pregnancy because he was their child, not ours, and if they wanted to keep him away from his grandparents, it was their prerogative. Jack's calling us liars in our own home—that was something we might talk about, maybe. But then at the end of the night, we decided we were going to let bygones be bygones and start from there, no apologies required. We didn't want to rehash everything. We wanted to move past it.

We arrived at Starbucks first, got our coffees, and sat down. Naomi and Jack arrived right after us, got their coffees, and sat down across from us. Kirk was not with them.

I jumped in. "Well, where do you want to start?"

"I have a letter I'd like to read to you, but I don't know." Naomi looked down at the folded paper in her hands.

"Go ahead and read it, Naomi. Be brave."

Lance and I were under the impression . . . well, Naomi had said she wanted to work it out between us, so I assumed the letter was an apology or maybe an explanation of the weirdness of the year. I was interested in what she had to say. I was hopeful for reconciliation and maybe even healing between us, especially between Naomi and me.

"Okay." She unfolded the paper and started to read.

> Mom and Dad,
>
> I love you very much. Remember that time we went camping and we were laughing so loud and it was so late that our neighbors came over and shushed us? I barfed up our dinner, and Dad buried it. Every camping trip after, Dad just made a preventive hole for me to barf in. I miss those parents. I feel you two are going down a destructive path that I cannot be around. You both have severe eating disorders that you refuse to get help for, and it breaks my heart.
>
> Mom, I feel that your eating habits have caused you to become so self-absorbed and neglectful of others that you have no control over your emotions or actions. You say mean and hurtful things to the people you say you love the most. There are times when I want to share something with you and I stop myself, knowing that I can't trust you to protect and validate my feelings because you condescend to what is important

to me. I miss those times when you used to play your guitar for me and we would sing together. I feel like we bonded and spoke the same language. Now I don't even know who you are.

Dad, I was really looking forward to going camping with you and Kirk, but with you having a sore leg and being on crutches as well as having diabetes, I believe that if you do not get help, your physical health is only going to get worse. I was looking forward to you and Jack taking Kirk on his first shooting trip when he's five years old, but I am not sure that you will even be alive or able to by then. You may be okay with dying so young, but those of us in your life who love you are not okay with it.

Thinking that you two are the only ones who are suffering from this is selfish. I am not okay just sitting by with my family and watching you live like this. I don't want my son to see people that he loves and adores so much hurt themselves in this way.

I feel that being an addict takes a lot of work. It is not for lazy people.

Mom, when you put so much effort into your food addiction, I see Kirk getting the leftovers of that. You are unable to control your tongue and emotions. It takes effort and work to control these things in a healthy way, and you cannot manage both.

Dad, in the same way, when you put your food addiction ahead of Kirk, you slowly lose the ability to play and wrestle with him, which is what he enjoys doing most. You are emotionally unavailable and unable to keep up with him and play with him. And it's not fair for Kirk to see you decline in that way.

I feel sad when I think that I can't have a relationship with you because your addiction to food is more important to you than me or my family. Unless you both get some help, I will not let myself or my family be around you.

Naomi

She handed me the letter.

Well, that is a slap in the face. What happened to working it out?

It was Lance who broke the silence. "So where do we go from here?"

"Like it said in the letter, we can't be involved with you until you get help," Naomi said.

Jack didn't speak at all.

"Okay." I did my best to remain calm. "So until we do whatever it is you want us to do, there's no contact with you or your family, right?" Disbelief—she was really going to blow up her family. I just couldn't believe she would do this to us.

"Right." She looked down.

"Okay. Well, Jack, take care of my daughter and my grandson," I said.

"Oh! I will!" He had a weird exuberance I'd never seen in him, like he was happy to be rid of us.

"We love you, Naomi. Goodbye." There was nothing else I could say.

They rose and walked out the door.

Well, good for him. He won.

Lance and I sat in silence. We sat there for ten minutes, twenty, maybe thirty—I'm not sure. Eventually, we made our way home, much less hopeful than when we had left just one hour before.

Chapter 36

So This Is a Thing . . .

After that day in March, I was depressed and angry and sad. I talked to all my friends, reading them the letter, and asking them for reassurance that Lance and I were not those people Naomi described. I cried about the bad mom I must've been to raise such an ungrateful, entitled, spiteful child, and I compared myself and Naomi to all the "good moms" and "good daughters" that I knew.

I couldn't talk about anything else but what Naomi had done to us. I told everyone I met. I told strangers I talked to in any line when they asked me about my kids. I'd tell them I had two daughters but that one of them was estranged, and "Let me tell you what she did!" I begged for someone to fix it, but all they could do was listen and be shocked and sad with me.

One Sunday, not long after the letter was read to us, I

went to church alone. Lance was on call and was working. After the service, I pulled into an empty parking lot and started to scream and cry to God.

"Fix this! God, I can't take this. You have got to fix this! Please, please, *please*, *please*, I beg you, fix this! I can't live like this. We don't deserve this. Lance and I were good parents. We gave her everything, supported her in everything! We do not deserve this! Please, God! Please!"

The longer I yelled, the more the panic climbed through my body. The realization of this relationship being broken for the rest of my life set in. I hit the steering wheel and screamed and cried and begged some more. I went on and on until I couldn't anymore, until I had nothing left—no words, no energy, no hope.

I put my head on the steering wheel and cried silently for I don't know how long, and then I sat up, wiped my eyes, and headed home. How was I ever going to get through the next fifty years feeling this way? Would it ever get better?

Once I realized this was going to be a thing in my life, I started looking for support. I joined a parent estrangement board online and started reading stories of other parents who had been discarded like yesterday's trash— stories that would make your head spin and your heart break.

The boy who called his mom on Mother's Day to tell her he didn't want to ever talk to her again with no explanation.

The daughter who wouldn't talk to her mother because she wouldn't give her money for the fiftieth time.

Parents get rejected and ignored for many reasons,

often because selfish adult children are not getting their way. Some of the adult children are mentally ill, some are in controlling relationships, and some are narcissists, but they are all estranging their parents and breaking their hearts.

Reading through the stories and the comments, I was amazed at the similarities to my own story and appalled at the injustices. I felt some comfort knowing I wasn't alone, seeing there were others who were dealing with these children who, for whatever reason, decided they didn't want or need their families anymore. The stories were sad and shocking, sometimes tragic. I spent hours a day reading and researching this thing called "estrangement" until I couldn't do it anymore.

I noticed about half—*a portion too large to ignore or write off as coincidence*—of the stories were the same as mine; moms who were close—*maybe too close, enmeshed, like me and Naomi*—with their children until they hit adulthood, and then the adult child walked away with little explanation, if any. The moms who were left behind were distraught, some of them surrendering their lives to the grief, staying in bed, giving up, letting their health deteriorate.

It was especially difficult when there were grandchildren involved. One lady watched her three grandchildren while the parents worked, and then one day, after years of her watching them for free, the parents decided she wasn't good enough to watch the kids. They took them, and seldom brought the kids to see her again.

Post after post chronicled painful losses and numerous attempts at reconciliation, to no avail. These parents were being thrown away, ignored, and treated like they didn't have a purpose. It was so sad. I read the board multiple times a day, desperate for a method or a plan for how to feel better, how to deal with all the emotions, or how to move on.

One day I read a post that got me off the board and into my life with a flash of insight. It was about this woman who said she had been healthy, had been involved in her church, and had friends and a productive life until her son called her one day and said he never wanted to see her again and she would not be welcome in her grandkids' lives.

She tried to reason with him and gave it time, but the longer it went with no response from him, the more she resigned herself to her new life and her new identity: a mother who had been rejected by her son. She stopped getting out of bed. Her cholesterol and blood pressure began to climb, not to mention the depression. She went from being a woman with an active life, taking no medication, to a woman who could barely get out of bed, taking many medications to keep her body alive.

I mourned for her. I tried to encourage her on the board to get up and get back to her life—to stop waiting for her son and her grandchildren. I wrote how her value was not in how much her son loved her but in who she was: a human being with friends and a future.

That was when it hit me. I had to get off this computer and back into *my* life! No matter how much I didn't *feel* like it. I would not let this situation kill me. No way!

So, after pouting and crying for months, I hired a trainer at the gym to give me a reason to get out of the house and get moving. I went three days a week, training with a lovely man from my church who was in his seventies. We would talk about Naomi and what she had done to our family, and he would tell me his adult son stories. I started to find out that many parents had problems with their adult children—even the "good parents," the involved parents. Although I didn't feel happy, I felt accomplished, and I continued to make my way through the sludge of estrangement.

Months passed with no word. Even though I got my body moving, the battle raged on in my heart and mind. Lance and I would talk about Naomi and her childhood and all the things we could have done wrong. I rehashed every bit of her life, trying to figure out what had happened. How did this sweet child of mine turn into a monster? How could she turn on us? She loved her family, she always wanted to be around us, and then, all of a sudden, "Get out of my life because you're fat"? We'd always been fat, and she had never seemed ashamed of us before.

The chatter in my mind went on and on, keeping me awake some nights, making me cry every day. It was consuming. I was obsessed. I just wanted to fix it. I wanted to reason with her—to have her get a clue. I kept thinking if I could lay it all out in front of her, she would change her mind, would make the right decision, and come back to us.

No matter what I could have said, no matter how much truth I threw her way, she was not going to get it. She had forsaken her family.

One morning I was working—I work at home on the computer doing data entry—when this strong, unrelenting feeling came over me. I had to write Naomi a letter. I had to ask her for forgiveness, and I had to ask her to meet me so I could read it to her. I was still in Celebrate Recovery, and making amends is part of the plan. I hadn't realized there was anything I had to ask Naomi's forgiveness for, but there was.

I sat down to write, and the words fell out onto paper. It was like it was already written, and all I had to do was get it down. It was a very strange experience. I believe the

Holy Spirit moved me that morning. The letter was done in minutes.

I texted Naomi as soon as I put the pen down.

> I have a letter I'd like to read
> to you. It's an amends letter
> about the way you were
> raised. It has nothing to do
> with you as an adult. I would
> like to read it to you in person
> without the men. If you
> won't allow me that, then I'll
> mail it to you. It will take 2
> minutes of your time and I'll
> meet you anywhere. It could
> be on your porch while Kirk's
> sleeping. If I don't hear from
> you by this time tomorrow,
> I'll drop it in the mail. Thx.

She agreed to meet me at the coffee shop by her house, where we had gone many times in the past. This was the place where we used to play canasta for hours. We loved this coffee shop. We knew the owners, and they knew us.

I arrived first, so I found a table and sat down. I smiled when I saw her walk in. She was noticeably pregnant this time.

I hugged her. It was lovely to see her face, and I was excited to see her, until the sadness made itself known.

She ordered her coffee and sat down across from me. I could tell she was nervous, so I got right to it.

"A friend of mine is watching Kirk, and I told her I'd be ten minutes."

"Okay," I said as I pulled out the letter. "I'm going to read this letter to you, and then I'll give it to you."

She nodded.

Dear Naomi,

I did not treat you like a child while you were growing up. I treated you like a friend, and even worse, as my savior. I lived my life through you, telling you exactly how to act and how to be. Because of this, I didn't allow you to develop your own personality, to be yourself. I tried to make you into this perfect person by trying to keep you from making any mistakes or doing anything wrong. I took your childish failures personally, as a reflection of me when you were just being a child and making mistakes to learn about yourself and your surroundings.

I wanted you to be the *do-over* of my life, of the life I coveted. You had everything I ever wanted. You had beauty, and you were thin, and you were talented. I wanted you to make the most of those things the way I would, not the way God made you to be and not how He wanted you to use them. I put way too many expectations on you, and I accept responsibility for it, and I am so sorry. You are God's perfect model of Naomi. You were never meant to be a duplicate of me, and I'm sorry I put that on you. I hope you can forgive me someday.

I also treated you like my savior, my acceptance, and my love. I put so much on that little baby when she came into the world—too much for any one person to handle. You were a child. You were not responsible for me feeling loved, accepted, or safe.

I am sorry for those times I yelled at you for being a kid. I know now, you didn't know any better. I'm sorry I scared you when I retreated into my room when I felt overwhelmed. I'm sure there are other things you can remember I messed up on, and I ask for forgiveness for those, too, because I know I wasn't a good mom to you.

From the moment I saw your face, I knew you were my answer. You were the love and acceptance I never had, and I held on to you as tight as I could. Children are not meant to fill our empty parts. They are not meant to serve us at all. I was the mom. I was the adult. I was the one who was supposed to love and accept you and serve you, and I didn't do that.

I hope you can find some way to forgive me.

I love you.

Mom

My voice broke toward the end. She showed no emotion.

I folded up the letter and handed it to her. "Naomi, is there any way we can make this better? Could we get a mediator or a counselor to help us work through this with one another? Dad and I are willing to try."

"Well, what about starting with an apology?"

"An apology for what?"

"For that night. For . . ." Clearly, she didn't know what for.

"Naomi, that's why we need a counselor. Someone to help us sort this out."

"We don't need counseling. We just need you to apologize."

"We can't apologize for something we didn't do. You can't even tell me what you need an apology for. How can *we* know if *you* don't know?" I asked evenly. "Naomi, I really think this problem is between the two of us. If you and I could get some counsel, together, I think we could work it out. I know I didn't parent you correctly as a single mother. Let's figure it out. Let's get someone to help us."

The conversation moved on to talking about Kirk and all the fun things he was doing. She told me how well she was doing in her life and how much she loved being a stay-at-home mom. We settled into a lighthearted, almost normal conversation, even getting comfortable enough to laugh together.

She had to go, so we ended it. I walked her out to the parking lot and hugged her tight.

"Please think about it, about getting counseling with me. Dad and I will pay for it," I said in a last-ditch effort.

"Okay, Mom." She pulled away. "I'll think about it and let you know. Maybe it would be better if we got some counseling."

I watched her as she got into her car and drove away, hoping the next time I heard from her, we could make an appointment that would move us toward reconciliation.

I received a text from her two days later.

> After seeing you yesterday,
> I realized that you haven't
> changed and that not having
> contact with you is the best
> thing. I have been really
> enjoying my life the last
> several months and I have
> gotten all of the counseling
> that I feel I need for now.
> When you two acknowledge
> the severity of your addiction,
> let me know, we can talk.

This was not Naomi's voice, and I knew it. We had gotten along fine at the coffee shop, we had talked, and we had even laughed a little. She had stayed for an hour

instead of ten minutes. She didn't think these things written in the text. I knew it, her dad knew it, everyone who
knew her and loved her knew it, but it didn't matter. She
was staying away.

The grief that overcame me after this encounter was
like nothing I'd experienced before. It wasn't like the
shock of losing my dad or the long-suffering of losing my
mom. It was a deep, penetrating soul wound. I was losing
the only thing that ever meant anything to me, and I was
not going to survive it. I didn't want to survive it.

Every day was excruciating to live through. I missed
her at every turn. She was my life, my purpose, and my
heart. And my heart had just stood up and walked away
without a second thought, without looking back. I meant
nothing to her, so I was nothing.

The enmeshment was so intense it took years to un-
ravel. I had friends who were good enough to walk me
through some of the lies and misconceptions I had about
my daughter and where she fit into my personage. I went
from coast to coast visiting my friends, trying to make myself feel better, thinking someone would have the answer.

Chad, in Maryland, reminded me Naomi was not *my*
Naomi—that she was her own person, and she was not
mine and never had been.

Mary, in Utah, nurtured my heart in my grief, but she
was also quick to tell me the truth when my hopelessness
would threaten to consume me.

Her husband, Bill, would come up with counsel at the
weirdest times, like the time we went grocery shopping
and I announced to him as we were getting out of the truck

that I had decided I couldn't be sad anymore, so I was going to write Naomi off and never think about her again. We argued all the way through Walmart. He encouraged me to keep my mind and heart open to reconciliation. By the time we hit the checkout, I was convinced.

He was also the one who, along with my husband, reminded me that God is the place to put my faith, not Naomi—not a person, never a person.

Then back home to my husband, who would listen and listen and listen to the same stuff until self-hatred spewed out of my mouth. That was when his tolerance ended, and he increased the volume of his voice to let me know he would not listen to me lying about myself, which resulted in me dissolving in tears.

No one had "the answer," but they all had *an* answer that I believe propelled me toward healing and a better understanding of myself and my God.

Another strong propulsion toward healing, one I believe was straight from God, came in the form of a letter from my friend Carol. She was not the kind of friend who gave advice. Whenever I'd tell her about the problems I was having with Naomi, she would simply say, "huh." It was a little irritating to me because, remember, I was trying to find an answer. I wanted someone to give me the magic words or thing to do to fix this relationship. Carol definitely wasn't the one to do that for me. She'd listen, but she wouldn't offer anything. That was so frustrating to me, but I appreciated having her ear.

Probably six months into the estrangement, I got a letter in the mail from Carol. It was handwritten on a note card.

Dear Michelle,

As I sat here praying for you this morning, I got a picture of you standing strong and sure, alone, but warm and embracing with your arms stretched out to Naomi. But you can't take the steps to her. You need to be still and let the H. S. [Holy Spirit] do a work in her. This is her battle against God, not against you, and He is the one doing the battle against the stiffness in her neck. You will be her comfort when she is done, but until then, you must give Naomi up. She will bend her neck, and when she does, a flood of pain and fear and remorse will wash over her. You will deflect that flood so she can rise up and be strong *with* you instead of against you. She does not realize who she is pushing against, but by you staying still, God can show her.

I see flowers in the desert all around you and encourage you to see the beauty, trust God, and wait. Still.

<3 Carol

I read those words over and over, letting the encouragement and hope sink in. I would pull the card out and reread it when I felt I couldn't go on one more moment. Those words were for me, for this momma's heart—and I loved Carol for sending them to me.

From God to Carol to me.

But as grief will do, it came in waves. The moment I thought I was done, it washed over me again.

The mourning flooded over me, making itself known in a mighty way. The tsunami of pain, the begging, the reasoning, the talking incessantly about it, crying and more crying—God bless my husband and my friends for putting up with me. When was this going to end?

I met with Lory to process through the pain of yet another rejection. We met at church an hour before CR began and sat together on a couch in the youth room.

"I just want to die. I have nothing left. No reason to live." My eyes were dry.

"Michelle, what about your husband? Lilo. Your friends. They would be sad if you died."

"They don't need me . . . they'd be fine without me. Naomi *needed* me. She was the only person in the world who truly loved me."

My voice broke, and the tears started to come in an avalanche of hopelessness and betrayal. "Why doesn't she love me anymore? She was my life! I was her life! How could she do this to me? I depended on her to be there when I grew old, to take care of me, to love me. Now I'm all alone. I have nobody. First my parents are taken away, making me an orphan, and now Naomi."

I crumpled into a ball on the couch, crying so hard I could barely breathe, then screaming into the pillow I found nearby. My insides felt like they were being ripped out of my body. I hurt everywhere. This spot in my heart where my daughter dwelled was gone, and I wasn't going to survive it. I really wasn't going to survive it. My heart was broken, and I wanted to die.

Please, God, take me now. I can't stand it anymore. I have no more reason to be on this earth. Please, God, please, let me die!

I'm not sure how long I had been in the whirlwind of emotions when Lory spoke up. I lifted my head out of the pillow and met her eyes.

She swiped a tear from her cheek, took a deep breath, and calmly said, "Michelle, you have a life separate from Naomi."

The screaming and yelling had stopped. Now there were only tears.

"God did not create you to live someone else's life. He created you with an individual plan in mind. Naomi has her own life, with her own plan. This world needs you, Michelle, for as long as God wills it. We need your joy and wisdom, your energy and friendship. There is a place for you on this earth, and you belong here. You, Michelle, have a reason to live."

"I just can't understand how she could do this to me. I feel so betrayed. She was my life."

"Naomi is a person, Michelle. She is fallible and broken like the rest of us. She is doing the best she can, and she needs the Savior just as you do. Naomi is not your savior. She is not your god or your identity. You are complete and whole all on your own. You don't need Naomi to be complete. You need to stand on your own, be your own person, because the world needs you, Michelle. The world doesn't need a second Naomi; the world needs the original Michelle."

It took me years to get it into my heart and mind that I am good enough being me. I had been living as if Naomi made me matter, gave me value, made me shine. Losing her, having her ripped out of my identity forced me to shine on my own. I had to remember who I had been before I grafted Naomi into my identity.

I asked my friends what they knew about me. I asked my husband and read about what God says about me. It was time to fill the Naomi-shaped hole with the truth about me—to reconstruct my identity from scratch.

Chapter 37

My Freedom Is Hers Too . . . If She'll Take It

*I*spent years talking about dying and wanting to die. I believe in God, I believe there's a heaven, and I know I am going, and I also know that it is much better than here—here, on this earth where people let you down and leave you and you are all alone. Having people, being related, connected, known—it's all a fallacy, a lie. We are all on this earth alone to figure things out on our own.

Why would I want to stay on this earth, where the pain is daily and the disappointments run rampant, when I can be in heaven with a loving Father who has loved me from the beginning of time? Plus, I get to see my parents and my best friend. I begged God to let me die. I wanted to get out of this drama called life. I wanted out.

Then one day, while I was asking God to take me home, a thought entered my head. *This life I gave you is a gift. You may not give it back. I decide when you're done with the gift, and you're not done.*

I let the reality set in. Life is a gift God gave me. He created me to be exactly who I am, and He has a plan for me, for my life, and for my death. Who am I to say when it ends or how it ends? Not me. I am not the giver and taker of life.

I submitted my life to God. No more talk of dying. Even though I didn't feel any different, I knew I had to continue my life as God directed me to. Naomi was not my purpose. God was my purpose, and He obviously had a plan for me. I wasn't finished yet.

It had been two and a half years since I'd seen or heard from Naomi. I knew she'd had her baby, and it was a boy, and they had named him Jonas. I found out through Facebook. One of her friends was a friend of mine on Facebook, and she was at the birth watching Kirk while Naomi was laboring and delivering. I saw pictures of them, sometimes, when others would post them. The new baby was a cutie. Blond hair, blue eyes. Looked just like his mother, and so different from his brother.

I moved back into my life and away from the chocolate and the television set. I got involved in my church doing various duties and teaching. I taught a study to young moms called No Perfect Moms.

We had about eight young ladies in my class who were struggling, as many moms do, with their identities and their children. One of the ladies, Denise, had three little ones under the age of three with a difficult marriage. I took her under my wing, and I helped her as much as I could.

One day she and I planned to meet at the mall so the kids could play while we talked. That morning, as I was getting ready to go, I saw that Lilo was up and dressed and getting ready to leave the house. When I saw her coming down the hall, I had a feeling she was going to meet her sister at the mall at the exact same place I was going. I can't explain how I knew, but I had a strong feeling I was going to see Naomi and the kids at the mall that day.

I didn't say anything to Lilo. I just finished getting ready and drove to the mall in anticipation.

I arrived at the play place and watched as my daughters and my grandsons made their way toward me. They didn't see me, so I waited until they did. Lilo saw me first, and then Naomi, following her stare, saw me next. I walked up to them and hugged Naomi and said hi to everyone. I didn't want to come on too strong with the boys because I didn't know if Kirk would even remember me, and Jonas and I had never met before.

Kirk stared up at me, so I said, "Hi! Do you remember me?"

"Yep!"

Yay!

Almost on cue, Denise and her three littles showed up beside me. I introduced everyone, and then Denise and I sat down in the play place while the kids played. We weren't there long before Naomi came over our way, following Jonas. Naomi and Denise started talking about water births.

Before I knew it, all of us had migrated to the merry-go-round. I stood next to the ride and talked to Kirk and Jonas, although Jonas didn't have a lot to say to me. I asked Kirk what he was doing these days and who his favorite superhero was. I can't remember the conversation because I was just so happy to see his little face. I loved that he remembered me and that he wasn't afraid of me and wanted to talk to me. I could have listened to that voice forever!

After a while, Naomi asked if we'd like to go on the train with them. We did, and I paid for everyone to go. Since there were so many of us, we would have to take two cars. Naomi got in one car with Jonas and Lilo. Denise got into another car with her boys. Kirk was walking alongside me.

"Hey! You wanna go with us?" I dared.

"Yes!"

Oh! My! Heart!

We got into the train car with Denise, and he talked my ear off. He told me about his dad and superheroes and his birthday and how many times he'd been on the train. I got the feeling he was wondering why I hadn't been at his birthday parties, and that made me sad for a minute. He was such a lovely boy. I loved him so much. I wished his papa could have been there to see him.

The train ride ended, and I said goodbye.

And I was okay. I wasn't sad. I told my husband about it and hashed through my feelings, but I was okay. I had accepted the relationship for what it was going to be. I didn't cry all night.

I might see them once in a while, I guess, if we happened to bump into each other, maybe? Anyway, I was happy to have seen Kirk and to have met Jonas. I was grateful for the gift that was given to me.

Days after I saw Naomi and the boys at the mall, I got

a text from her asking me if I'd agree to see her counselor with her. I was glad to.

The first visit with the counselor was interesting. Naomi and I met in the lobby, and when the counselor came out to see us, he didn't remember I was coming. We sat down in his office, and he asked Naomi why she wanted me to come to the appointment with her. She said something like she wanted to talk things out and how she didn't really want anything to do with us except for holidays.

Honestly, I don't remember much more about that first visit.

It wasn't until I got home that I realized the counselor didn't know about the estrangement or anything pertaining to us, Naomi's parents. She must not have talked about us. I had a hard time believing he didn't ask about us, because every time I've been to a counselor, the first thing they ask about is your family of origin. So why didn't she talk about us or the estrangement? Why else would she go to counseling?

I arrived at the second visit ready to inform him of our history. I even brought the letter she'd written. If Naomi wasn't going to tell him, I would. We were wasting our time and money in that office if this counselor didn't know the history.

I sat down and took control of the meeting. "I am going to tell you our history because I don't think you know."

"Okay, that's fine." To Naomi: "You all right with your mom starting out?"

Naomi nodded.

"Well, it all started when Naomi's grandmother died— my mom. Naomi was old enough to start working, and she wouldn't work. Her dad and I encouraged her to get a job, and she just wouldn't. Finally, her dad made her work eight hours a day around the house until she got a job. It took one day, and she got a job."

I took a breath and looked at the counselor, then down at his pen as it scribbled across the page. I looked at Naomi. She was sitting perfectly still.

I told him how our relationship had changed from being close, to her punishing and ignoring me at every turn. I explained how we watched the baby until they didn't need us anymore and how they disowned us because we were fat or addicted or needed to apologize. I gave him the whole picture from the beginning, and I rolled it up in this final analysis:

"I think Naomi is mad at me for abandoning her when she was two. She was shipped off across the country to spend six weeks with her dad and his wife. Naomi was not familiar with them, as they'd had nothing to do with her for half her life. Since she was such a resilient child, a happy one, I assumed at the time she would handle these separations fine, but now I don't think she did. I think it did some damage, and when her dad and I started to push her out of the nest, encouraging her to get a job and to be an adult, I think she took that as us, or particularly me, abandoning her again, and she's been angry at me ever since."

I stopped for a moment and smiled. "That's my opinion on what happened."

I'll never forget what the counselor said next.

"Uh . . . um . . ." He stuttered, keeping his eyes on the paper in front of him. "I didn't know any of this stuff."

It seemed like he was talking to himself. I noticed his face was flushed, and . . . was he angry?

Looking up at me, he continued, "This is all new to me."

Wow! So I was right. Huh.

I realized I was staring, but before I could pull my eyes away from him, he said, "Um . . . well, you are very good at this analysis stuff. You're not a counselor, right?"

"No," I said, looking at Naomi. "I just know my daughter."

The counselor finished writing, and then he turned his attention to Naomi. "Naomi, you are not ready to have a relationship with your mother." He looked at me. "Naomi isn't ready. She needs more counsel, in light of this information."

I nodded. "So, to be clear, you are saying you don't want me and Naomi to have any contact with each other?"

"Yes, that's what I'm saying. Naomi is not ready."

Really? How is that healthy? More separation. That doesn't make sense to me.

We walked out of the office together and stopped at the sidewalk to talk a bit. Naomi told me she was going to Overeaters Anonymous, and it was helping her. I asked her if she'd be willing to meet once in a while for coffee, maybe once a month, and she said she would think about it. We hugged and got into our cars.

See? We can do this. That therapist doesn't know what he's talking about.

I was halfway home when I got a call from Naomi in my car.

"Hi!"

"Mom. I believe you have borderline personality disorder, and my family cannot have contact with you until you get help for it."

"Naomi." I chuckled. "I do not have a borderline personality. I took abnormal psychology, and I do not have the traits of a borderline."

First I'm a liar, then I'm too fat, then I'm addicted and so can't be trusted with their child. Next, they need an apology for something they don't even know, *and now I have BPD. I have had enough of her accusations. I am not even hurt. This is ridiculous.*

Oh! The therapist was right, she isn't ready. Wow. Okay.

"Well, I think you do," she said, "and until you get help, you can't be in our lives."

"Okay! Bye!" I hung up the phone and went home. No drama, no tears. I was done.

Eight months passed. Lance and I were sitting in the kitchen after dinner one night when a text came from Naomi to her dad.

It was a picture of the boys holding stuffed animals. Then another text:

> You guys should stop being
> mad and come play with us!
> We just won some prizes . . .
> gonna go on some rides . . .
> then eat funnel cake . . . MY
> TREAT!

Subsequent texts went as follows:

> at pv mall

and

> Ps. Jack isn't here . . .

and

> I'm persistent so you can't
> ignore me forever . . .

Lance and I discussed it and decided it wasn't a good idea. Lance texted back.

> It would be nice to see you
> and your family, however, I
> don't think it is a good idea
> for us to be in and out of the
> boys' lives.

From Naomi:

> Yeah, I didn't think an
> occasional carnival visit would
> kill them, but I def understand
> where you guys are coming
> from if you didn't wanna
> come. I thought mom said
> something about reaching
> out, so I asked. I'm trying
> this 'don't overthink it, go
> with my gut' thing, lately. It
> was fun, we were laughing
> and enjoying ourselves and
> I thought randomly, "hey, I
> should see if the folks wanna
> hang." I'm too old and I'm
> too tired to remember the
> rules or hold a grudge lol.
> Thanks for texting back and
> have a great night. I hope you
> enjoy the weather while it
> laaaasts!

Obviously, she didn't feel any responsibility for the way she treated us or the things she accused us of.

Our next conversation was via text when Naomi asked if she could come by and pick up Kirk's pet lizard. Naomi had decided she didn't want the lizard anymore, so she had given it to Lilo to keep. She wanted the lizard back as a potty-training bribe.

We were sleeping in that morning and didn't get back to her soon enough, so she sent a second text using uncharacteristic profanity. I just smiled and rolled my eyes when my husband read it to me. She couldn't hurt me anymore.

When she came by the house, she sat for a couple of minutes and told us what was going on in her life. She told us she had left Jack! She was living in a friend's apartment while he was out of town. The apartment was small and in a sketchy area of town filled with drug addicts and ex-cons.

She still didn't offer explanations or apologies or make an acknowledgment of the pain she had inflicted all this time. Lance and I didn't need an explanation from her for her behavior as much as we were curious about what was going on in her mind during this time—what caused her to turn against her parents, seeing us as the enemy instead of seeing us as her advocate?

Chapter 38

So, Yes . . .

We let her and the boys back into our lives. We wanted to be forgiving and love unconditionally, like the father who took back the prodigal son, but we were detached and cautious in our approach to them because any time they left our house, we didn't know if or when we'd ever see them again.

Early on, I tried to talk to her about the pain she had caused us, but she wouldn't talk about it.

She'd throw out comments like, "I know. I'm sure my boys will do the same thing to me," or, "Yeah, I know, Mom."

Never a "sorry" or any type of remorse. It baffled me.

One time in the car, I approached the idea. "Don't you feel like you need to apologize to us?"

"Why? Do you think you *need* an apology?" She spat out the words.

"No, I don't need one, I guess. I just thought you might want to clear your conscience, clear the air. But I guess if you don't feel like you need to . . ."

During the months following her return, Lance and I would often talk about how surreal the situation was. We didn't know her anymore, and the boys didn't know us. We felt like we were in the twilight zone, going through the motions, knowing we should be engaged with these people, but feeling separate, disconnected.

One afternoon after Naomi and the boys left, I plopped down on my chair to talk to Lance.

"She could decide to go back to Jack, and we'd never see them again."

"I know."

"Well, then I'm not going to get too close to those kids. I am not going to go through that again. No way!"

"That's your prerogative, but you could make some memories with them while they are here."

"They probably won't remember. Especially Jonas. He's so young."

"I know. You do what you can live with. We have no control, Michelle. They are their kids, not ours. We get what they give us."

"I hate that! It's just not fair!"

Variations of the same conversation transpired often during the first year after she came back. She talked about going back to Jack many times, so we never knew what our future as grandparents would be.

The month after she sent that first text was Kirk's birthday party. I couldn't go because I was out of town, so Lance went on his own. He called me that night to tell me about it.

"It was at a kids' play place where they had snow and ice and stuff. I didn't go into that part. I stayed in the party room. It was just so weird. People were pleasant enough, but the boys didn't have much to do with me. They just don't know me. The whole thing felt like a dream, like I wasn't sure if I belonged there. I kept thinking how we'd been told for years how we're too horrible to be alive, and now I'm sitting at my grandson's birthday party. It was surreal."

"Yeah. Sounds like it. I'm sorry you had to go without me."

"It was fine. Jack apologized to me."

"Really? What'd he say?"

"It was an apology, but not really an apology, apology." He chuckled. "He said, 'I'm sorry if anything I said offended you.' And that was it."

Naomi and the boys would come over on Sundays and have dinner with us. One Sunday, she was leaving to go to a party at her apartment complex. A sense of dread came over me.

"Naomi, be careful around those people."

Before I could go any further, Lilo countered, "What do you mean 'those people,' Mom? Because they're poor?"

"No. It's because I smell pot every time I go to her apartment, and I have had more than one encounter with drug addicts. I've heard yelling and cussing. It's not a safe area. That's all."

Lilo rolled her eyes, and Naomi assured me. "Mom, it's not a big deal. We'll be outside by the pool. It's fine."

Naomi had been involved with this group of people, and she would tell me stories of them taking advantage of her kindnesses, asking for rides and money and babysitting. I tried to encourage her to step away, but she wasn't interested in my interference.

"Okay. Have fun." I was resigned.

One night late in June, at about ten thirty, I was sitting on the couch chatting with Lance about the day. My cell phone rang, which was unusual in our home at that hour unless something was wrong. The caller ID read "Naomi."

"Hello?" I answered tentatively.

It was a man's voice. "Hello, Mrs. Rohlf? This is Officer Anderson from the Phoenix Police Department. We have your daughter here in her apartment, and she seems to be under the influence. She called 911 saying she was afraid she was being chased, and she was hiding under the bed. Since she wouldn't come to the door, we had to kick it in."

"Um . . ." I didn't know how to respond. "Is she okay?"

"As far as we can tell. The paramedics were here and took her vitals. She seems to be fine, but she wanted me to call you. We cannot leave until you get here."

"Okay, thank you. We'll be up there as soon as we can."

Drugs? She's doing drugs now? What is wrong *with this girl?*

I drove us to the apartment in silence, except for the one time my husband asked me to slow down.

"The police are going to stay until we get there. No reason to rush," he said calmly.

We walked through the dark corridor to her apartment. A young girl ran up to me and asked if Naomi was going to be okay. She was one of the children Naomi had babysat.

"I don't know, Honey. We just got here."

The policeman met us at the door. "We got her out from under the bed."

We followed his gaze to the chair in the living room where she was . . . sleeping? Unconscious? Not sure. She was coiled up, like she'd rather be in the fetal position but there wasn't room.

The apartment was a mess. There was half-eaten McDonald's food on the counter. Every corner was stuffed with things—boxes from moving, toys on the living room floor, dishes in the sink, trash on the floor. The woman police officer interrupted my assessment of the place.

"Where are her kids?" she asked, accusingly.

"Oh, right. They're with their dad. They're safe." I assured her.

I could tell the woman police officer was irritated—just another drug addict not living up to her responsibilities. I wanted to explain to her how Naomi wasn't that kind of person. How she didn't do drugs as a rule and how she was a very good mother, but I didn't. I heard the male policeman talking to Lance about the door and how they needed to wait for their supervisor so he could take pictures and document the breakage.

Once the police officers had left the apartment, Lance went to fix the door. Naomi was still sort of slumped in the chair, not moving, not speaking.

I looked around the apartment and took it all in. Such a mess. *How can she live like this?*

And then my better angels kicked in—*she needs help. This woman needs our help.* Maybe I could get a couple of my friends to help her organize the house. I knew what it was like to leave your life and move into a whole different one when you're depressed and alone. I would help any woman who was in this situation, so why wouldn't I help my daughter? *I'm going to contact some of my friends and see if we can make her and the boys' living situation better.*

My thoughts were interrupted by my husband. "Michelle, could you please hold this molding right here?"

We finished securing the door, gathered Naomi, and started toward the car.

Naomi was able to walk under her own power with a little help from her dad. I told her she was welcome to move in with us if she wanted to get out of that apartment complex. I didn't say much more because I didn't know how much she would remember, but it was important to me that she knew she had a place to go. My parents had given me somewhere to go after my divorce, and I had always been thankful for having a safe, soft place to land.

On the drive home, I heard her mumble something about her life being over and that she wanted to die.

I turned off the radio. "Naomi!"

She slowly raised her head to meet my eyes.

"Are you suicidal? Do you want to kill yourself? Is that what you're saying? Because if you are, we are coming up on a hospital right now, and we can pull in there and get you admitted. So tell me. Are you thinking of hurting yourself? Tell me *right now.*"

"No, Mom. I'm fine," she muttered, turning toward the window and watching the hospital as we passed by.

We got home and tucked her into bed. I reminded her once again she could move in with us. I didn't know if she would remember my offering, but I had to try.

She didn't take me up on it.

Chapter 39

A Return to the Nest

About a month later, Naomi and I were talking in the parking lot after an event. She looked tired and stressed. She said they had moved and were living in a house with eight other people. She complained about the environment for the kids and how things were just crazy.

Lance and I had been discussing how we could help her and the boys ever since that night with the police. We had offered our home to her multiple times, but she always refused. I offered again, and she said she would think about it, again.

Soon after that conversation, I left to spend some time in Utah with Mary. I tried to get up there as much as I possibly could, especially in the summer when the daily temperature stayed between 105 and 115 in Phoenix. I longed for the 80s or even 90s of the Utah mountains. Sometimes

I drove the ten hours—I love a good drive—and sometimes I flew. This time I drove. Driving was therapy for me, and I definitely needed some.

I was headed home after my lovely time in Utah with my friends when I received a text from Naomi. I pulled into a gas station and read her message.

> Would you and Dad let me
> and the kids move in for a
> while? I think the kids would
> feel safer with you.

I took a deep breath, relieved she was making a responsible choice. She was *finally* asking. I texted Lance, and with his answer, I returned her text.

> Sure. You and the boys are
> welcome.

Naomi and the boys moved into the house, making my nice, clean, uncluttered home into a chaotic mess of boxes and furniture. The more stuff she brought over, the more anxious I got. I kept my mouth shut the best I could, but I had a hard time coming home from work to a living room full of boxes and every surface filled with stuff. I kept reminding myself it was only going to be this way for a week or two, but it wasn't.

Naomi struggled with what to keep and what to get rid of. She was mourning the loss of her house and the home she had built with her husband. Almost every "thing" she considered became a major decision as to whether to keep it or give it away. She had a story for why she had bought it or how it had come about.

I was irritated with how long it was taking her to sift

through her crap, mostly because I am not a "things" person, and I couldn't understand why she couldn't just keep what she needed and get rid of the rest. But eventually, I realized these things symbolized the life she wanted for herself and had thought she had. Each "thing" she had to give up was like giving up a little more of her dream. Although I didn't understand it, I could see her agony.

She had been in the house for a week or so when she came into the kitchen to talk to me. Lilo had come over to the house to use the computer, but in hindsight, I'm pretty sure it was a strategic move. Lilo was at the house to provide Naomi with support.

"Mom, I need to tell you something."

I wiped my hands and turned around to look at her. "Okay. What's up?"

Shifting from foot to foot, she nervously drummed her hands on the island.

Oh crap. What now?

"I don't want to tell you," she said, more to herself than to me. Then she yelled, "Sister!"

Lilo came running down the hall to stand beside her.

"Just tell her," Lilo encouraged, but before the sentence was completely out of her mouth, I knew.

"You're pregnant."

"Yeah, I'm pregnant."

"By who? Who's the father?"

"I don't know, Mom," Naomi said, and then at the speed of light, the story tumbled out. "I think it happened that night with the cops. You know, the night you and Dad picked me up at the apartment?

"After that day, I didn't want to live there anymore. I didn't know why, except I was scared to go home. So I packed us up and moved to my friend Jasmine's house. I had been there a while when Jasmine said she thought I was acting pregnant. I said I couldn't be pregnant because I hadn't had sex in a year, but she brought home a pregnancy test the next day, and it was positive. I hadn't had a period for a while, I guess, but I didn't think about it because I'd been so stressed. So, well, I guess I was pregnant. The test was positive. That's why I moved away, I guess. I didn't know why I didn't feel safe at that apartment anymore, but I knew I couldn't be there anymore."

I was quiet, listening, processing all the information as it rained down on me. *That's why she was so afraid that night. She was hiding under her bed because she had been raped, but she didn't know, and she didn't remember. What is she going to do with that baby? She is barely hanging on with the two she already has.*

I pulled myself out of my thought storm. "Do you have any clue who the father is? Who did you see that night?"

"Mom! I don't know! I went to a party in the apartment complex. And after a while, I noticed I wasn't feeling great, so I went to my apartment to lie down." She was quiet for a moment, staring somewhere past me. "I wasn't thinking clearly. I noticed that, and then I remember seeing a form standing in the doorway, blocking the light through the front door. The next thing I remember was the policeman coaxing me out from under the bed."

"Do you think you were drugged?" I knew the answer. "I'm so sorry, Naomi."

She shrugged.

"What are you going to do?" My head was spinning.

"I don't know. All I know is I need to keep my boys and this baby safe. That's why I had to come home."

"Are you keeping the baby?"

"I haven't decided. I will probably give it up for adoption."

"Okay. I guess there's no hurry to decide. It's still really early."

We stood in silence, staring at each other but not really seeing each other. I realized Lilo was no longer standing next to Naomi. She had gone back down the hall sometime during the conversation.

Naomi started to walk away.

"Wait! Who's going to tell Dad?"

"You can." She walked down the hall.

I turned back to the dishes and processed this new information the same way I did most things—slowly. This was her life, and I didn't have any control over how she was going to handle the assault or the pregnancy. All I could do was support her the best I could, as much as she would allow. We had another life coming into this world.

Thank you, God, for this sweet baby. Keep it safe and help it grow. Amen.

Sometime after they moved into the house, I noticed how Kirk was keeping his distance from me. His affection was detached, and he wouldn't talk to me any more than he had to.

One day it occurred to me that he was mad at me for leaving him. We had gone from spending his first two and a half years together, seeing each other three times a week, to not seeing each other at all. I'm sure his little brain had a hard time reconciling this important relationship, especially when he had no control over it. I had been there, and then I wasn't.

Or maybe he thought he had done something wrong

that made me leave him. They say children think every-thing is their fault, that the world revolves around them, and I could see how he might internalize rejection because of my absence. It was either his fault or mine, and I'm sure it was easier for him to make it mine than to understand how it could be his.

I asked Naomi if she would talk to him for me because I thought he felt abandoned by me, and she agreed to talk to him.

That night when it was time for the boys to go to bed, I got an exuberant hug and cuddle from Kirk. He let me hold him as he told me about his day, something that had not happened since they had come back into our lives. When Naomi returned to the living room from tucking the kids into bed, I asked her what she had said to him, because whatever it was, it had worked.

"I just told him that sometimes moms and dads make bad choices, and that it was our choice to stay away from Mimi and Papa, not Mimi and Papa's choice. I told him you and Dad loved them very much and always wanted them."

Chapter 40

Finally—Some Responsibility

Naomi needed a car because she had totaled hers some time before she had come home. She had money from the sale of her house due to the divorce, so we found a nice, well-maintained car for her.

The day she bought the car, we were on the way to her bank to get the money when I spoke up. "I want to be involved with this baby, since I didn't get to be involved with the others."

"Mom, I don't know. I think it's going to be really hard for you to let this one go, especially if it's a girl."

"I won't have a hard time, Naomi. This is your baby, not mine. I will respect whatever you decide to do. I would just like to be a part of the process."

Ultimately, I was involved in very little where the baby was concerned. She didn't tell us much about what was going on in her life or her head. She stomped around the house being angry and unhappy without talking to us about what was going on and was, sometimes, almost unbearable to live with. She continued in her pattern of blaming me when things didn't go her way. I don't think she was even conscious she was doing it.

One example of her chaotic behavior happened the night after she bought the car. We were all sitting around in the living room—Naomi, Lilo, me, Lance, and my friend Kassie. It was about ten o'clock, and Kassie and I had just gotten back from picking up a piece of used furniture for her to refinish. We were talking and laughing and actually enjoying ourselves when I announced to the room, intending to encourage my daughter, "Today Naomi got a new car for a good deal. She got a job. She has it made!"

"Oh, yeah." She scowled at me. "So I have it made, do I? I'm pregnant with my rapist's baby, and I have to figure out what to do with it! I really have it made, *Mom*!"

The words exploded through the room like a bomb, shrapnel raining down. My eyes immediately flew to Kassie, who was sitting next to Naomi. I watched Kassie's face as some shrapnel found her. Her face registered shock first, then embarrassment—or maybe that was me projecting—and then compassion. Knowing Kassie, compassion came quickly.

I was irritated. Naomi wouldn't talk when I tried to get her to talk, and then when she did, she exploded all over the room.

The next six months continued much the same way—silence interspersed with foot stomping, anger, and prolonged absences with no explanation of where she was going or how long she would be gone. I knew she was an adult, and I didn't really care where she was going. I just wanted to know who was in my house and at what times. We asked her multiple times to respect that rule, but she wouldn't follow any of our rules. She'd tell us the first time after our conversation, but then she was back to no communication.

We finally decided to accept it the way it was, reminding each other that she wouldn't be living with us forever. Sometime soon she would find her own apartment and be on her own, hopefully sooner than later.

This was hard.

Come January, Naomi still hadn't made a decision on what to do with the baby. The baby was due in just eight or nine weeks. I talked to her about it as much as I could, and sometimes she would actually communicate what was going on in her head.

I think she was set on placing the child for adoption from the beginning, but she didn't want to face it until she had to. There would be many families interested in this healthy, white female baby, but the timing had to be right for all those involved.

My friend Tiffany, who had adopted three of her four babies, was heavily involved with the adoption community. She had a friend who was ready to adopt a second, but the timing didn't work out. Then Tiffany found another person she had talked to online and felt they might be a good fit.

This family had had two adoptions fall through and one successful adoption—a little girl who was three years old. Naomi was sent the adoption book and profile so she could learn about them and their history. She became convinced this was her baby's family, and they set up a meeting.

Naomi invited me along the day she met them in person. We met in a restaurant, all of us—Naomi, Lilo, me, the prospective family, and two social workers. The family was lovely. I could see the woman would be an attentive, doting mother, and the dad was much the same. They talked about their big extended family and all the love this child would receive.

I could see my granddaughter growing up with them.

I wasn't included in the delivery, same as with the other two babies. We received a text from Lilo hours after it was over, letting us know it was all done and everyone was fine. Naomi had a water birth, like she did with the boys, but this time she had to do it at a birthing center instead of in her home. Naomi graciously allowed the adoptive mother to get right into the water to catch the baby, lifting the perfect baby girl to her chest. The adoptive father leaned over the water to cut the cord.

They named her, and she was grafted into their family.

A week later, my husband and I were invited to meet the baby. I wasn't sure about meeting her. I didn't know how I'd feel about seeing her, holding her, and loving her, then never seeing her again, but curiosity trumped my uneasiness.

Our whole family went together, as well as the grandsons, to a place in the city. It was an unusual place located in an old home. They sold coffee and pastries in the living room, and then in the backyard, there were picnic tables, a play structure, and lots of toys for the kids.

It was the perfect place for us to meet our granddaughter.

They handed me the baby. Lance and I took turns holding her. The adoptive mom gave Naomi some presents. I watched as she opened them. I watched the adoptive dad play with the older sister and thought he would be a good dad to this baby girl too.

I breathed in the morning air, sat back against the fence, and wondered how I'd feel in the coming years when I remembered I had a granddaughter out there growing up and living her life and having nothing to do with us. I decided I'd be fine. Knowing she was well cared for and loved would be enough. Observing her parents, I believed she would grow up in a loving family with God as the center.

I reached out to my husband and took the baby from him for one last time. I watched her and cuddled her close, willing myself to memorize her face. I said goodbye to her in my heart and my mind and said a little prayer for her life. I handed her to Lilo.

Smiling, I settled into my peace. I knew she would have a lovely life. She was going to be okay, and so was I.

Naomi had moved out and back in twice since her divorce, and the last time she promised she would get a job, save money, and get her own place in a year.

She didn't work for the first few months, and since it was right after her delivery, I was willing to give her some time to heal. However, a few months turned into many months, and I started feeling used. I realized we, my husband and I, were enabling her. We were allowing her to stay at our house rent free with no obligations. Every time she moved into our house, it took months for her to get settled, and every time she moved out, she'd leave a mess behind.

This time—this *last* time—it was months and months before she organized the back room for the kids and the bedrooms for the three of them.

We do not live in a large home, but there was room for everyone to have their own bed. Naomi would stay up all night with the TV on and fall asleep on the couch. The light from the TV interrupted my sleep, and I would go out and turn things off at 3:00 a.m., irritated that she was not paying the electric bill.

Finally, after eight months of living in our house, she got everything situated. The kids had their own TV in the back room so I could watch shows without worrying about their little ears, and the bedrooms were the way she wanted them. The last thing was for her to get a job.

"Mom, I am going to move into Jane's house for two weeks to see if it works for us."

"What? Are you kidding? Naomi! You just got settled here. Why are you going to move again?" I complained.

"I told Jane if her room became available to let me know so I could move in. The people moved out, and she needs me to make a decision."

"What money are you using?"

"I have money, Mom."

"Naomi, please, don't do this. You just got settled here. You have a chance to get ahead if you just get a job and save some money, and then you can find something bigger than one big bedroom for all of you. I can't believe you are considering moving your boys again! They've moved five times already since you left Jack. That is not good for them. You must know that."

It didn't matter what I said. She moved out.

I was happy to have my house back, but I had wanted to believe her when she moved in the last time and said she was going to work and save money and make a life for her and her boys. I had so appreciated the help my parents gave me when I was a single mom, and I wanted to pass it on, but it wasn't working the same for Naomi. She wasn't getting better. She was still making the same bad decisions, and her money was running out. I knew her dad and I would be the ones who'd have to pick up the pieces when she imploded . . . again.

Then there was the whole conversation about whether we would help her or not. Tough love and all that. But then there were the boys, and how much would we allow them to suffer so Naomi would learn a lesson?

Lance and I grappled with those things daily, and sure enough, the time came when Naomi needed money for car repairs, a ride from the car place, and a ride back to get her car. She eventually needed us to take the boys so she could go to school. She finally got a job for ten hours a week, minimum wage. When her car broke down again and she didn't have any money to her name, Lance and I paid for it, again, but at least she had started working. We also gave her money for lost credit cards, forgotten bills, and late charges.

Grr.

I know these are things we do freely for the people in our lives. It's just that I so much wanted her to get it together and make a life for herself. Every step back—a lost credit card or an unpaid bill—magnified the fact that she wasn't growing up, and if she wasn't progressing, we were going to have to help.

I felt like I was never going to be free from the responsibility of taking care of her, and recovery required I stop enabling her.

People will say we shouldn't have enabled her by paying for car repairs or helping with bills and such, but we couldn't bring ourselves to leave her entirely alone to figure it out. It would have been easier—that might not be quite the right word—maybe, for her and for us, if she lived farther away, but we were close. We *could* give her rides and watch the boys. I could never come up with a good reason why not. There were plenty of reasons to help. Such a balancing act!

It was a quandary.

When she left that last time, I realized I had to tell her she could not come back. I begged her to reconsider, to stay and get a job and save the money, to take advantage of this time and get ahead. I really wanted to give her a boost so she could make a future for herself and her boys like I did for myself when she was the baby. But she had to do it her own way, and like everything else, it wasn't the same way I did it. I guess that's growing up, after all.

I want to make one thing clear. I didn't tell her she couldn't come back to be punishing or hurtful. I told her she couldn't come back because I was not going to go through the upheaval in my home one more time. She had brought so much chaos into our home the last couple of years. I was not going to do it anymore. I had to be true to myself, and having her in, out, happy, sad, angry, silent did not create the home I had worked for.

I was glad, for myself, that she left, because enabling her in her inaction was not conducive to my recovery. It didn't seem to be an ideal choice for her, but then again, maybe it was.

Naomi finally started school for medical billing and coding. We—mostly Lance—took the boys almost every day so she could go to school.

This was a stressful time for me because I was back to not having my peaceful, clean house to myself again. The boys were there all the time, and when she wasn't in school or working, she was there too. I was so irritated that she had a home, yet she still camped out at our house.

I kept going back to that conversation I'd had with her about *not* moving out and how if she had stayed with us she could have saved money and it would have been easier to watch the boys with their beds here, and on and on. But in the end, she was not growing by living in her childhood home, and maybe she knew she wouldn't. So it was a good thing she moved out.

God knew what would get her moving. I didn't.

Chapter 41

The Promised Land— Does It Exist?

N aomi and the boys went to a different church than we did, but she came to our church services when her church was closed for the pandemic of 2020, sometimes with the boys, sometimes without.

One morning, Lance and I were in church when the pastor showed a picture of a fish, its head still on, with some french fries. He was talking about the Red Sea and showing this plate of food called the St. Peter's dinner.

I heard my phone buzz, so I picked it up—I know, habit—and it was a text message from Naomi.

Just like Europe. Yum

I had no idea what she was talking about and went back to listening to the sermon. Then the phone buzzed again.

☺ ☹

then,

Right behind you

I did not know what the heck she was talking about, so I put the phone away and finished listening to the sermon. When the sermon was over, I talked to some people and turned toward my husband. He was holding some little boy.

That seems strange, I thought. We didn't know anyone well enough that he'd be holding . . . then I realized there was a little boy climbing toward me in the pew, and it was my grandson.

Oh! That's what Naomi meant! She was there, in the church, behind us. We had fish with heads on when we went to Europe.

Everything fell into place. I was so used to not having them around, it didn't even cross my mind that they were in the church. Jonas said hello to me and then inched himself down the pew toward his papa.

I stood a couple of feet away and watched my family interact, Papa holding Kirk, and Naomi picking up Jonas from the pew as they talked to each other and those who passed by them. I closed the distance between us and reached up to tickle Kirk's belly.

"Hey!" I said to Naomi. "You all wanna go to lunch? I'm thinking Mexican."

"Yeah, sounds good, Mom."

Outside, I stood at the steps as I watched Naomi and

her boys walk to their car. I realized I felt happy. This is the way it's supposed to be to have adult children. We come together to share experiences, and then they go home to their lives, and we go home to ours. This was what I had always wanted, and maybe we were actually on our way.

Chapter 42

My Happy Ending

Here's my truth.
I have loved movies and television for as long as I can remember. The television was a constant presence in our home growing up. My mom watched soap operas all day, then when Dad got home it was news, *Wheel of Fortune*, and *Jeopardy*. After dinner we would retire to the living room and watch prime-time television. I have fond memories of my parents in our living room laughing at *M*A*S*H*. These days whenever I hear that theme song, I am transported back to 1972.

My mom started dropping me off at the local movie theater in our small town as soon as I was old enough to be on my own. She would let me see any movie with a G or PG rating. Unless it was a movie that I understood, I usually went just for the socializing and the candy.

One time when I was fourteen, my friend and I took the bus to see *Star Wars*. We spent the entire day watching the movie over and over again, living on licorice and soda. That day is one of my favorite movie memories.

Why am I telling you all of this? Well, because I always wanted my life to be like the movies or the thirty-minute sitcom. I want to see the resolution in situations and relationships. I want to see forgiveness and reconciliation and redemption.

The man who finally realizes it's his best friend he truly loves, not the perfect model he's been dating.

The dad who resents his son's love for ballet because he's always wanted a son who played football, but Dad shows up to the son's ballet recital and ends up hugging the boy and saying, "I'm proud of you, Son."

The mother and daughter who can't find common ground for the entire two hours until the final scene, where they finally come to an understanding and the daughter sees that Mom isn't that different from her.

The perfect ending: understandings met, conflicts resolved, justice dispensed, amends made, relationships restored.

Fade to black, credits roll.

This hasn't happened for me. No resolution, no explanation, no relationship restored. Naomi didn't automatically appreciate her parents once she became one. She didn't humbly ask for forgiveness when she came back into our lives, even though we welcomed her. She didn't offer reasons for running out that Christmas, for writing us that awful letter, or for staying away for years. When she finally acknowledged her role in the damages, it was indirect. There was a beginning, a middle—but no *end*.

No fade to black, no credit roll.

So it is my job to find resolution for myself. What can I live with? How can I fit this relationship and the history surrounding it into my reality? She says she doesn't remember many of the things she put us through—the rejection, the letter, even the "counseling" I attended with her therapist. The fact that she can't remember makes the relationship feel unsafe to me. If she doesn't remember, does that mean she might do it again? Possibly. How can I invest in a relationship with my daughter and her children if I could lose them again at any moment? She didn't value us enough to fight for us the first time, so what says she won't desert the relationship again?

One thing I've learned over the past ten years is that there are no guarantees. The only things I can control are my own choices as life happens. I have to move forward with what I have in front of me right now. I can't live the rest of my life in the what-ifs. What-ifs rob me of the joy I have for today. I can invest in my grandsons' lives and my daughter's life for the time I have them. That's all we have anyway, right?

Life is not a movie. It's not a hundred and twenty minutes of love, conflict, complication, climax, and resolution, fade to black. Life is years of imperfect people trying to find their way in this crazy world. I have this moment. I'm responsible for my life, and it's my choice to give love and acceptance. That's where my power lies.

So I will not wait for an apology from Naomi or for her to realize the error of her ways, because I could be waiting a lifetime, and what a waste of time that is. I'll love her and her boys in this moment. I will love them for the time I have them in my life, imprinting them with love and acceptance.

What about me? I'll be all right. I don't need anyone to rescue me or a knight to love me. I am finding my own happy ending. I know who I am, and I know I have purpose. Forward!

Fade to black, credits roll.

ORDER INFORMATION

REDEMPTION **P**
P R E S S

To order additional copies of this book, please visit
www.redemption-press.com.
Also available at Christian bookstores and Barnes and Noble.